Be scientific

Contents

Discussing	1.1
Planning	1.2
Recording	1.3
Presenting	1.4
Applying	1.5
Classifying	1.6
Evaluating	1.7
Experimenting	1.8
Hypothesizing	1.9
Inferring	1.10
Interpreting	1.11
Investigating	1.12
Observing	1.13
Predicting	1.14
Questioning	1.15
Be scientific – some useful words	1.16

Symbols you will find:

► These are things you should
try to do.

These are extra things to do
if you have time.

These are questions to think
about when you are
planning practical work.

When you see this symbol
you need to take extra care.

This theme contains 15 spreads
which can be worked through **in
any order.**

Theme 1

Discussing

When you are learning, it is very important to talk to other people and discuss things. This helps you to get your ideas clear in your head. Scientists often discuss their work with each other, and you need to do this in your work.

You will learn a lot from listening and talking to each other. Talking and listening are an essential part of everything you do in **Science in Process**. You will usually work in groups of three or four people.

Discuss

▶ Get into a group of three or four. Do Cut Out BS1 (part 1). Make sure you try to do all the things in the picture below.

Record

▶ Write down the order you decide on – you will need it later.

Discuss

▶ Discuss each point in this checklist. How good was your group at discussing?

| Did everyone get a turn to say what they thought ? |
| Did everyone listen to each other's point of view ? |
| Did everyone have something to do? |
| Did everyone agree with the decisions the group made? |
| How did you come to a decision ? (Vote, agreement ...?) |
| How could you improve next time ? |

Discuss

▶ Ask your teacher for Cut Out BS1 (part 2). This has information about how much electricity each appliance uses.
▶ Now discuss in your group the order for the cut strips that you decided on before. Do you want to change it now that you have this information?
▶ Go through the discussing checklist again. Have you got any better at discussing?

Record

▶ Record your new order.
▶ Record any ways you have got better at discussing.

Discuss

▶ If you wanted to reduce your electricity bill, which appliances would you use less often?
▶ Imagine you are moving to a place where you can only get 50 units of electricity a day. If you could take five appliances with you, which ones would you take and why?

Planning

When you are using **Science in Process** you will often be asked
to plan, or follow a plan. 'Follow the plan' means you will
have instructions to follow. 'Plan' means you will have to
decide how to do the activity yourselves. Use the flow charts
to learn how to plan your science work.

How to follow a plan

Read all the information given and look at the diagrams. Watch out for any care symbols ⚠

↓

Discuss what you are trying to find out. What do you already know that will help you?

↓

Make sure you understand what to do. There may be exact instructions, or there may be practical questions with a ◆ symbol to help you.

↓

Make sure you read the **Record** before you start. What does it want you to do? What notes will you make to help you?

↓

Decide what equipment you need.

↓

Share out the jobs for this activity in your group.

↓

Now do the activity.

↓

If you can, try any activities with a ▶ symbol.

Follow the plan

You can use a circuit with a light bulb and battery to test
whether materials let electricity through. This is called
'conduction'. If the bulb lights up then the material
conducts electricity. You may find Skill Sheet 3 helpful.

Touch the two crocodile clips together to check the circuit.
Now put the aluminium foil between the two crocodile
clips.

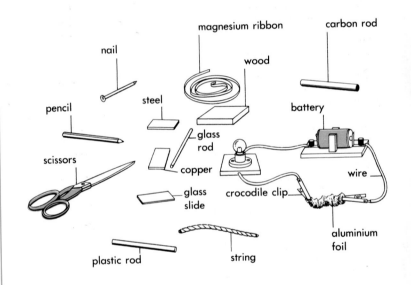

◆ Does the bulb light up?
◆ Does aluminium foil conduct electricity?
◆ What happens to the bulb when you put some of the
   other materials between the crocodile clips?

▶ Find out which liquids conduct electricity.

Record

▶ Make a list of the materials that conduct electricity.
▶ Make a list of some everyday objects that you think
   would conduct electricity.

Sometimes you will have to make your own plan and decide
how to carry it out. Use this flow chart to help you.

How to make a plan

Discuss what you are trying to find out. What do you already know that will help you?

Decide on a method to use.

Decide what things you can vary or change. Decide which things must stay the same for a test to be fair.

What things are you going to notice or measure?

What senses can you use? Is there any instrument that will help you?

⚠ Is your plan safe? Show it to your teacher.

Decide what you will record.

Now follow your own plan.

If you can, try any activities with a ▶ symbol.

Plan

Some metals fizz when they are put in acids.

Find out which of the metals you have been given fizz the most. This equipment might help you.

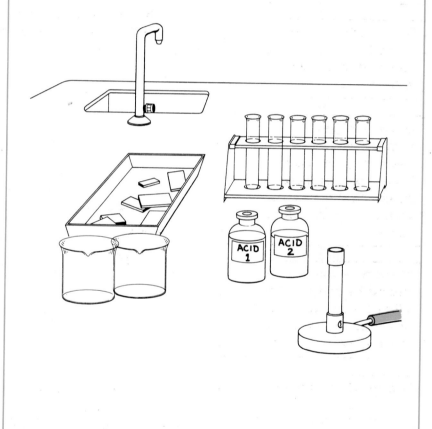

◆ What will you record?

Record

▶ Record what your plan was.
▶ Record what you found out.

Recording

You will do a lot of recording in science. You will need to record the things you notice. You may also need to record ideas you have so that you may use them again.

There are a number of ways you can record. The way you choose depends on what you need the recording for.

Plan

Your group is going to use the 'iodine test' to find out which foods have starch in them. Starch is a chemical which can give you energy.

Before you start, remember to read the instructions and think about which type of record you might use.

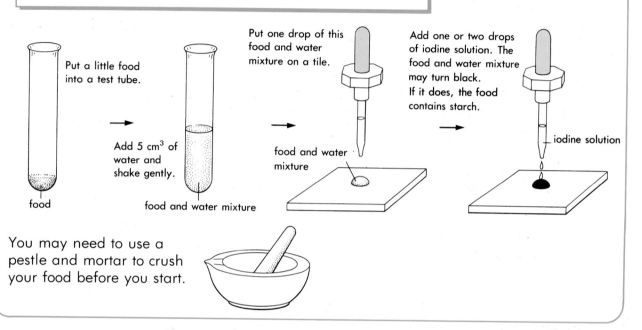

Put a little food into a test tube.

food

Add 5 cm³ of water and shake gently.

food and water mixture

Put one drop of this food and water mixture on a tile.

food and water mixture

Add one or two drops of iodine solution. The food and water mixture may turn black. If it does, the food contains starch.

iodine solution

You may need to use a pestle and mortar to crush your food before you start.

Record

▶ Make a table to show which of the foods you tested had starch in them and which did not.

The recording you have done so far will remind you what happened when you did the iodine test. You may also want to record other ideas or information about your results. To do this you will need to record what you did and what you found out.

Record

What we did

▶ Make a record of what your group did. Use Cut Out BS2 to help you.

What we found out

▶ Look back at the first record you made of your results. Decide what you found out.
▶ Write about 'What we found out'. Use one or both of the ways shown here to help you.
▶ Try other ways of recording.

We found out that if food contains starch it ....
If food does not contain starch it ....

Foods
starch   no starch

Presenting

Presenting means showing your ideas and work to other people. You can do this in a variety of ways. For example, you can make posters and charts, design and make models, or write and give a talk. You can write a play or story or poem and perform some of these, or make tapes or songs.

How you present something depends on who your audience is and where you are making your presentation.

Plan

You are going to collect some information about your teeth. You can then present it in different ways.

Use a mirror to look at the teeth in your mouth.

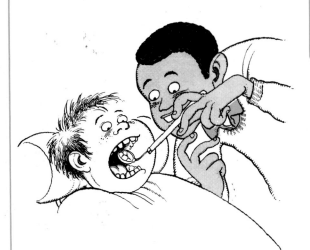

Imagine you are eating an apple or a piece of bread.

◆ How many teeth have you got altogether?
Look at the types of teeth shown below.
◆ Where in your mouth are your incisors, canines, premolars, and molars?

◆ What job do you think each type of tooth does? Some words you can use are: cutting, tearing, grinding, crushing, ripping, biting.

Types of teeth

Record

▶ Make a list of the different jobs each type of tooth does.

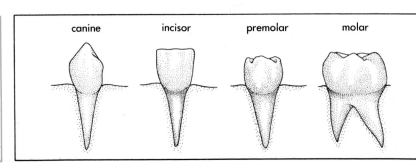

canine   incisor   premolar   molar

Present

▶ Use Cut Out BS3 to make a poster that shows the position of each type of tooth in your mouth. Label each type and colour it.

▶ Choose one or two other ways to present the ideas you have about teeth. There are some ideas shown below.

Before you begin, decide who your audience is and where you are going to present your ideas.

Making a poster

Making a model

Displaying your work

Always think about:

How much room have you got?

How big can your display be?

Are you going to use words, pictures, colours...?

Writing a story
You can write a story, poem or a diary about a day in the life of a molar tooth.

Molar's misery

My life as a molar
Is a real misery
I must crush and grind
When food I do see.

If the bits in my tooth
Are not brushed away
It won't be that long
'Till I'm full of DECAY.

DECAY is my ENEMY
Its making me rot
Destroying my friends
All that I've got.

So please treat me
Kindly
Or I won't last long.
Clean me often
And I'll stay strong.

Think about:

Who the story is for.

The jobs the tooth does.

What happens to the tooth during the day?
e.g. eating, drinking, talking, singing.

Doing a play

No more sweets for you.

This won't hurt a bit.

Aaarrgh!

Giving a talk

Taping

You can make a tape of your story for another group - or perhaps a song about your teeth.

1.4

Applying

Applying means using what you know or have found out in a new situation. In this spread you will learn about birds' feet and beaks and then **apply** the information by using it in another situation.

Birds' feet

Read this information. It tells you how birds' feet help them to live in their environment.

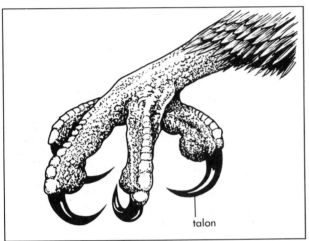

talon

Feet like this belong to a bird of prey. They are used for gripping and killing.

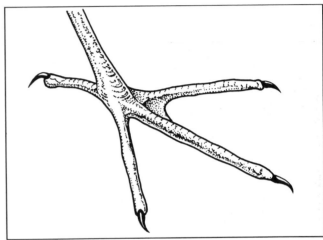

This foot has very long toes with small webs between them. It helps a bird stand on mud.

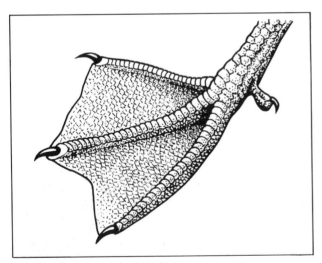

Webbed feet help birds to swim.

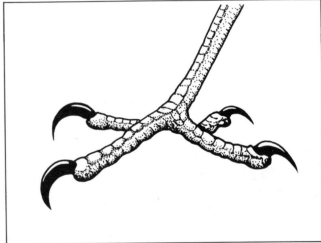

Feet like this one help birds to hold onto trees while they peck their food.

Birds' beaks

Record

► Do Cut Out BS4 to learn about birds' beaks.

Working out what birds eat

Discuss

You have now found out about birds' feet and beaks.
► Use this information to decide what type of food you
  think an owl, a gannet, a woodpecker, and a parrot
  would eat. You will be **applying** your knowledge.
► Use reference books to check your decisions.

Record

► Record your final decisions about what type of food
  you think an owl, a gannet, a woodpecker, and a
  parrot would eat.

Discuss

► Use what you know
  about birds to decide
  what sort of bird might
  live in this
  environment.
  Think about how it
  would walk around,
  what it might eat, and
  how it could hide. You
  will be **applying** what
  you know.

Present

► Design and draw a
  coloured picture of
  your bird.

Classifying

When you put things into groups because they are alike you are **classifying**. You can **classify** things in different ways. Sometimes you may use size, smell, colour, or shape to **classify**.

Classifying everyday things

The Hanlon family had a junk drawer in their kitchen. They used to throw everything into it. They decided to try to order it by dividing it into sections.

Discuss

Look at the objects in the Hanlons' drawer.
▶ Put them into the following groups:
  1 metal objects
  2 plastic objects
  3 paper objects
  4 any other objects.
You have now **classified** the objects.
▶ How useful is this **classification**?
▶ **Classify** the objects in more useful ways.

Record

▶ Make a record of your most useful **classification**.

Classifying living things

There are so many living things that it is useful to **classify** them. You can do this in different ways.

Discuss

▶ **Classify** the animals in Cut Out BS5 into two groups.
▶ What other groups can you put them into?

Record

▶ Make a record of how you **classified** the animals.

Classifying leaves

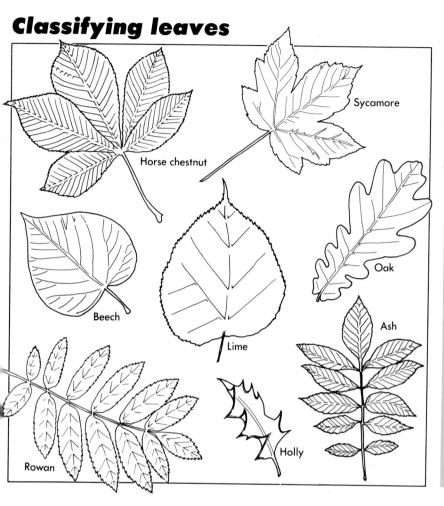

Horse chestnut

Sycamore

Beech

Lime

Oak

Ash

Rowan

Holly

Discuss

▶ **Classify** the leaves into two groups, those with smooth edges and those with toothed edges.

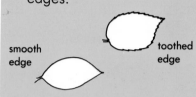

smooth edge

toothed edge

▶ **Classify** them into 'simple' and 'compound' leaves.

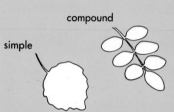

compound

simple

▶ How else could you **classify** them?

Using a classification key

A 'key' can be used to **classify** an unknown object. In keys, large groups are divided up into smaller groups by asking questions.

Record

▶ Make a record of your different **classifications**.

Discuss

▶ Look at the key and decide what animal X and animal Y could be.
▶ Make a key like this one to **classify** plants or vehicles.

Present

▶ Make a poster of your classification key.

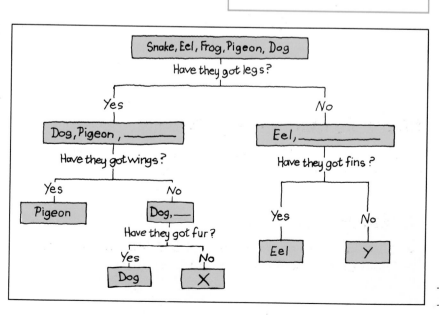

Snake, Eel, Frog, Pigeon, Dog

Have they got legs?

Yes

No

Dog, Pigeon, —————

Eel, —————

Have they got wings?

Have they got fins?

Yes

No

Yes

No

Pigeon

Dog, —

Eel

Y

Have they got fur?

Yes

No

Dog

X

1.6

Evaluating

Evaluating means judging the activity you have just done and deciding if it was fair or if you could do it better. Carry out the activity below and then **evaluate** what you did.

Plan

Test the strength of some carrier bags.

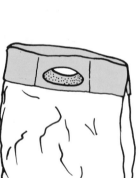

Look at the carrier bags.
Put them in the order of strength you think is correct.
◆ How will you test them?
◆ How will you record your results?

Record

▶ Make a record of what your group did.
▶ Use Cut Out BS6 to **evaluate** what you did.
▶ Make a record of ways you could improve activities you do in the future.

Discuss

▶ Discuss the questions on the checklist on the opposite page.

Checklist to evaluate your work

All the answers will be 'yes' for a perfect activity!

Did you make a safe plan for your activity?

Did your group think clearly about the idea you were setting out to test?

In your plan, did you decide what you would notice and measure?

In your plan, did you decide what you must keep the same and what you should vary to make your activity a fair test?

Did you have ideas about what you thought would happen, which you could then test?

Did you decide how to use the apparatus safely before you needed to use it?

Did you notice carefully what happened?

Did you make a suitable record?

Did you repeat the activity to check your results?

Did you discuss what you found out?

Did your results confirm your original idea, or help you change your idea to make it better?

Did your group work well as a team?

Experimenting

You will often have ideas about why something happens. When you test out your ideas you are **experimenting**. Before you **experiment**, you always predict what you think will happen. Check that you understand what 'predict' means. Spread 1.14 is about predicting.

Yvonne's group had been making different shaped boats in their CDT lessons. They had this idea:
'The speed a boat travels depends on the shape of its hull.'
The group predicted that:
'Our pointed boat will go faster than our rectangular-shaped boat.'

Plan

Plan an **experiment** to test this prediction.

Decide on some boat shapes to test. Draw them on centimetre graph paper before you cut them out.

Cut the boat shapes from a rectangle of polystyrene foam. Make sure they all weigh the same.

Leave one boat shape as a rectangle. This will give you a shape to compare the other boats with.

Check what you need to record *before* you do the **experiment**.

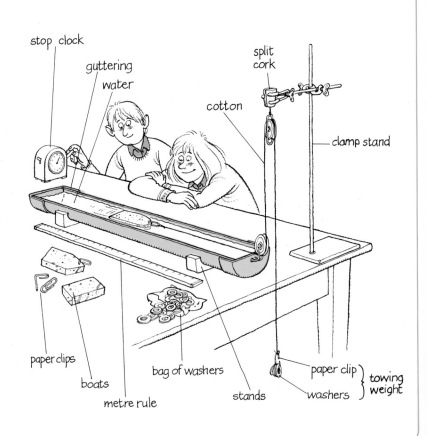

Record

▶ Draw the shapes you have made.
▶ Put the boat shapes into a list with the one you think will go fastest at the top. This is your prediction.
▶ Explain how you made all the boat shapes weigh the same.

▶ During the **experiment**, record the time each boat shape takes to travel along the gutter. Make sure you measure the same distance for each boat.
▶ After the **experiment**, record how your group's results agreed or disagreed with your previous list.

Discuss

Yvonne's group did this **experiment** too. They found out that pointed boats go faster than rectangular boats. Then they predicted that:
'Boats with pointed fronts and rounded backs go faster than boats with just pointed fronts'.

▶ Does your group agree or disagree with this idea?
▷ Test this idea if you like.

Follow the plan

Ben's group thought that the towing weights affected the speed at which the boats travelled. They decided to change the towing weight.

Predict what you think will happen.

Now test your prediction. You will be **experimenting**.

Time how long it takes to tow one of your boat shapes along the gutter. Do this three times to get a more accurate answer.

Now increase the number of weights towing the boat and repeat the test.

Take enough readings so that you can plot a graph.

▶ Shape of Boat

Weight Washers	Time in seconds			
	1st reading	2nd reading	3rd reading	Average
0				
1	6 sec	7 sec		
2				
3				
4				
5				
6				

Record

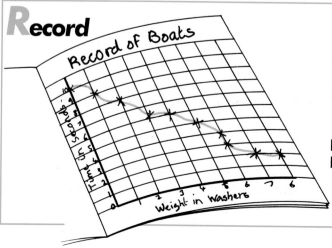
Record of Boats

Time in seconds
Weight in washers

▶ Make a table of results for your boat shape.
▶ Work out the average time for each trip along the gutter. Ask your teacher for help if you need it.
▶ Plot a graph (like the one on the left).
▶ Record whether your results agree or disagree with your prediction.

Hypothesizing

Making hypotheses

In science, you will often notice things happen. For example, you may notice that water from the tap on your bench flows downwards. You might then have the idea that 'water *always* flows downwards'. This idea is a **hypothesis**.

You might also have an idea which explains *why* something always happens. For example you may think 'water always flows downwards *because* gravity pulls it'. This is an even better **hypothesis**. **Hypotheses** are ideas about things which *always* happen.

Look at the diagram below. You can see Philip **hypothesizing**.

Yesterday my personal stereo stopped working properly.

Today I bought some new batteries for my stereo.

Now my personal stereo works again!
I have an idea!

Personal stereos **always** play properly when they have new batteries.
This idea is my **hypothesis**

Discuss

▶ In your group, think of an idea which explains why milk always lasts longer in a fridge. This will be a **hypothesis**. 'Because' and 'always' are useful words to use when you **hypothesize**.

▶ Think of an idea which explains why ice left in a room turns to water. You will be making another **hypothesis**.

▶ Do you agree with Philip's **hypothesis**?

Record

▶ Write down or tape your group's **hypotheses**.

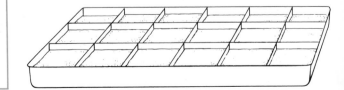

Testing hypotheses

When you have made a **hypothesis** you can test it. Usually you say what you think will happen when you do the test if your **hypothesis** is right. This is called making a prediction. The test you make is your experiment. You will find out more about predicting and experimenting in spreads 1.14 and 1.8.

Hypothesis	Prediction	Experiment
Personal stereos always play properly when they've got new batteries.	My friend's personal stereo doesn't play. It will if I put new batteries in.	Oh dear! It still doesn't work. There must be something wrong with my hypothesis.

Emma's group was finding out about paper falling to the ground. They noticed that a crumpled piece of paper fell to the ground more quickly than a flat piece. They had this idea:
'Crumpled paper always falls faster than flat paper'.
This was their **hypothesis**.

Discuss

▶ Do you agree with their **hypothesis**? If not, what ideas does your own group have?

Plan

Test Emma's group's **hypothesis**.

◆ How can you test it?
◆ What do you think will happen when you do the test?
◆ How many times will you do the test?

Record

▶ Record what you *thought* would happen.
▶ Record what *did* happen.
▶ Suggest your own **hypotheses** about the way paper falls.
▷ Try to complete this **hypothesis** 'Crumpled paper always falls faster than flat paper because ...'

Present

▶ Make a poster to explain to other people in your class how you made and tested your **hypothesis**.

Inferring

Suggest what is going on

Police are not often present at the scene of an accident so they cannot see for themselves what has happened. They have to work it out later from the evidence they find. Working out what has happened in this way is called **inferring**.

On Cut Out BS7 you will find some pictures. There are some statements about each picture too. Some of these tell you things you can actually see. These are observations. Check that you know what an observation is. If not, spread 1.13 will help you. Some of the statements try to suggest what has happened, even though you cannot see it for yourself. These statements are **inferences**.

> Two cars have crashed. This is my **observation**.

> I think that one of the drivers shot the lights. This is my **inference**.

Discuss

▶ Do the exercise on Cut Out BS7.
▶ How could you test whether your decisions were the right ones?

Inference boxes

Plan

You are now going to do some detective work of your own. Each box contains something. Without opening the box, you have to suggest what is inside it. You will be **inferring**.

Use as many senses as you can.

You may want to extend your senses and use a scientific instrument.

Think of different ways of affecting the things inside the boxes.

Only try one thing at a time.

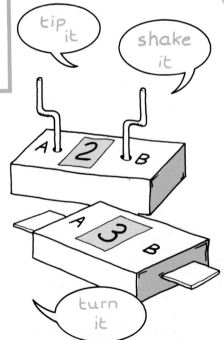

> tip it
> shake it
> squeeze it
> turn it

Record

► Make a labelled drawing of what you **inferred** about the inside of each box.
► Make a table to show what you did to each box (the cause) and what happened (the effect).
► Record which of your senses were the most useful.

Box	Cause	Effect	Senses used

Plan

▷ Design and build an inference box of your own. None of the sides should be longer than 10 cm.
▷ Try your inference box on a friend.

What is inside an oil drop?

Follow the plan

You are going to make **inferences** from the way a drop of oil behaves.

Place the bowl in a tray on a flat surface and fill it with water until it overflows.

Use a ruler to push off any excess water.

Sprinkle some fine powder on top of the water.

Dip a pin into some oil so that you get a *tiny* drop on the end.

Dip this into the middle of the bowl.

Watch what happens.

Try to measure the effect with some more drops. You may need to use clean water. Or you could try a drop of detergent instead of oil.

Discuss

► What did you notice?
► Suggest what happened. You are **inferring**.
▷ Imagine you are an oil particle. First you are sitting in the bottle of oil. Then you find yourself inside the oil drop. What happens next?

Present

▷ Write a story about the oil particle's travels.
▷ Use drawings to show what you think is going on.

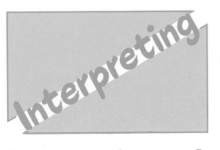

Interpreting means making sense of information. In science, you will **interpret** information presented in many different ways. It may be on graphs, in tables or pictures, or in words.

Interpreting at home

Below you can see some labels from clothes. Next to them is a chart which tells you what each symbol means.

Discuss

▶ Use the information in the chart to work out what the labels mean.
You are **interpreting** the information on the labels.

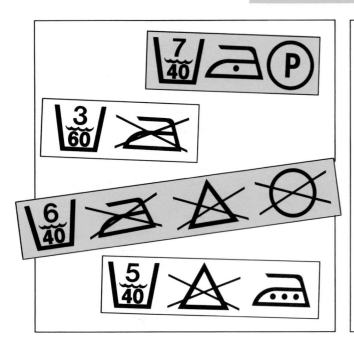

Maximum temperature 60°C

Do not use bleach

Do not machine wash

Use a cool iron

Use a hot iron

Do not dry clean

Dry clean

Record

▶ Draw each of the labels and write down your **interpretation** of each one.
▶ Write out the statements below and draw the correct symbol for each one.

Machine wash at 50°C.

It needs a special solvent so take it to the dry cleaners.

Use a cool iron.

Do not use bleach when you wash it.

Discuss

▶ What does this label mean?

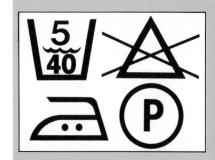

Interpreting in science

One group tried to find out how water travels along different materials. You can see the apparatus they used in the photograph. The results they got are shown in the graph below.

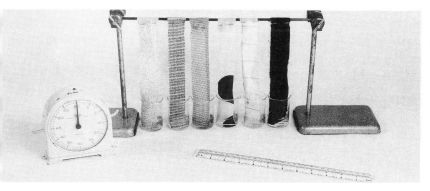

Discuss

Interpret the photograph:
▶ What do you think the group were trying to do?
▶ They measured each piece of material. Why did they do this?
▶ What did they use the stopclock for?

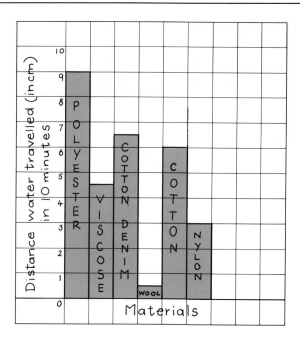

Record

▶ Suggest a title for this graph.
▶ Complete these sentences:
Water travelled furthest along _____.
Water travelled least along _____.
▶ Order the materials with the one in which the water moved the furthest at the top.
You have been **interpreting** the information on the graph.

Discuss

▶ Use the information in the graph to decide which of the ideas below you agree with. You will be **interpreting**.

Viscose and nylon materials absorb a lot of water.
Cotton materials absorb a lot of water.
Denim absorbs more water than viscose.
Cotton materials absorb less water than wool.
Polyester materials absorb less water than cotton.

▶ Decide how you could test each idea.

Investigating

When you **investigate**, you gather information about a topic. You can do this in a variety of ways — by using your senses to notice things, using instruments, reading, and talking to people.

Doing a survey

You are going to do a survey to find out how people choose their brand of washing-up liquid. You will be **investigating** how people choose what to buy.

Discuss

▶ Discuss some reasons why you think people buy the washing-up liquids they do. (Or, if you prefer, choose another product, such as shampoo or washing powder.)

▶ How could you find out how people choose washing-up liquids?

One way is to use a questionnaire.

▶ What questions would you ask in a questionnaire? Here are some ideas:
'Which washing-up liquid do you buy?'
'How much does it cost?'
'What do you like about it?'
'Who buys the washing-up liquid in your household?'
'Who uses it?'

Record

▶ Design your own questionnaire.

Plan

Now you are ready to do your survey. Your teacher will help you to duplicate your questionnaire.

◆ How could you use the questionnaire to survey your class?

◆ How could you survey the whole school?

◆ How could you survey the public? Decide with your teacher what survey to carry out.

Present

▶ Make a poster that shows the results of your surveys.
▶ Collect some empty bottles of washing-up liquid to use in your display.

Taking your investigation further

Discuss

▶ Look at some bottles of washing-up liquid and at some advertisements for them. What claims are made about each product?
▶ How do these compare with the results of your survey?

Record

▶ Decide how to record all the information you collect. A table like the one below may help you:

	Brand name	Cleano	Dazzle
claim	Smells nice	✓	
	Makes your hands soft		✓

KEEP YOUR HANDS SOFT WITH GENTLE KLEENO

Let the bubbles do the work with High Power Superclean

SUPER WHIZO IS SUPER CHEAP!

New Formula MAGIC is twice as POWERFUL

Plan

Choose one of the claims to **investigate** further.

◆ What are you going to notice or measure?
◆ What equipment do you need to carry out the **investigation**?
◆ How will you record your results?
◆ How will you make this a fair test?

Record

▶ Write down the claim you tested.
▶ Record what you did.
▶ Record what you found out during your **investigation**. Decide whether you agree with the claim.

Present

▶ Display what you have found out in a chart that the whole class can look at. You could suggest which brand you think is the best value.

Observing

When you **observe** in science, you use four of your senses to notice things: sight, touch, hearing and smell. You do not taste things in a laboratory because many chemicals are dangerous.

Plan

Use your senses to find out about each substance.

- What colour is it?
- What size is it?
- How does it feel?
- What sound does it make?
- What shape is it?

You are **observing**.

Record

▶ Make a table of your **observations** like this one.

Discuss

▶ Which **observations** would help you most if you wanted to describe the differences between the substances?

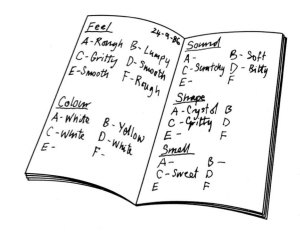

Measurement

Sometimes, in science, making **observations** with your senses is not enough. You need more accurate information, so you use measurement.

Plan

Find out about the substances you have been given by measuring them.

We could find the mass of a bottle-top full of the substance.

We could use a thermometer to measure their temperatures.

Which substance will make the highest pile when it is tipped onto a piece of paper?

◆ Which measurements will you make for each substance?
◆ Did you make your measurements as accurately as possible?

Record

▶ Make a table. Draw three columns and head them 'Height of pile', 'Mass', and 'Temperature'. If you can, put the substances in order in each column.
▶ Record which measurements you think told you the most about the substances.

Changes

In science you will sometimes do things to make objects change. When you are doing this, it is important to **observe** the object before, during, and after the change. Use as many of your senses as possible. It is also very important to measure how long each change takes.

Plan

Choose one of the substances provided. Make this substance change and **observe** the changes.

Some changes

If you add water to the substances some of them fizz.

If you add vinegar to the substances some of them fizz.

If you add iodine some substances turn it black.

◆ What changes could you try. Some ideas are shown on the right.
◆ What will you measure before, during and after the change?
◆ Who will **observe** and who will record? Different people should do this.
◆ How will you time the changes to the nearest second?
◆ Try these tests on other substances.

Present

▶ Design and make a label for each substance so that when it is on a shelf it can be easily identified. Use the **observations** you have made for each substance.

1.13

Predicting

People make **predictions** all the time. The children in the picture are making a **prediction**. If they catch the bus they can feel happy with their **prediction**. If they do not catch the bus, they must think about why their **prediction** was wrong. Your **predictions** depend on the things you notice and what you already know. If you do not know anything about a situation you cannot make **predictions**. You can only make guesses.

We'll catch the bus if we run.

Discuss

Here are some questions for your group to answer:

Will it rain tomorrow?
Will there be a full moon tonight?
Will school be open tomorrow?

▶ Ask each person the questions.
▶ Decide which answers they give are guesses and which are **predictions**.
▶ Make a list of some information you could collect that would help you to turn your guesses into **predictions**.
▶ Test your **predictions**.

Making a sensible guess

Sometimes, you will make a **prediction** that is wrong because something unexpected occurs. For example, you might **predict** that school will not be open on Saturday. But this particular Saturday, the school might be open for a festival. So your **prediction** would be wrong. Sometimes, you may not be able to find any information that will help you make a **prediction**. Then, you have to make a sensible guess about what you *think* will happen.

Plan

Try these activities, which both involve making **predictions**.
You can do either one first.

Fill your container to the top with water.

Predict how many 1p coins you think you will be able to put into the bowl before it overflows.

Test your **prediction**.

- ◆ Can you give a reason for what you noticed?
- ◆ Would you expect a similar result with a tall, narrow, glass container?

Container A contains small marbles.
Container B contains large marbles.

Predict which container, A or B, you think will need more water to cover the marbles.

Test your **prediction**.

Make sure you measure the amount of water you pour in.

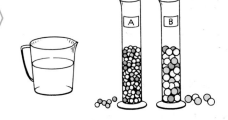

- ◆ What do you think would happen if you used sand instead of marbles?

When you test **predictions** you are experimenting. You can find out more about experimenting on spread 1.8.

Discuss

Look at the table which shows the average height and weight of all the students in the first four years of a secondary school. Four readings have been left out.
▶ **Predict** where they should be placed in the table.

Age	Boys height (cm)	Girls height (cm)	Boys weight (kg)	Girls weight (kg)
11	144	145	35	36
12		152		40
13	155	158	42	
14	163		49	49

38	150	45	160

Questioning

You will often need to ask **questions** to find out more about something you want to understand. Asking **questions** can help you to notice things and decide what sort of tests to do.

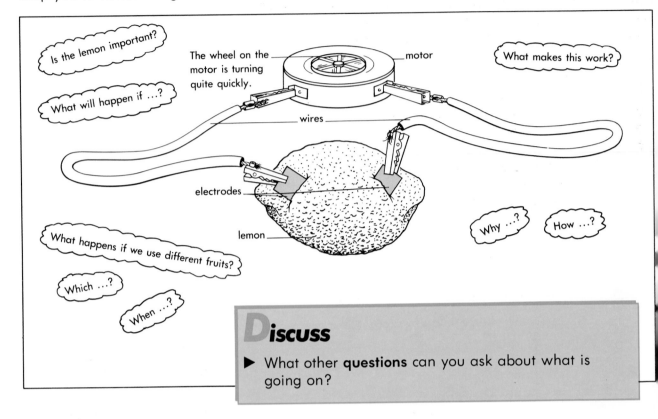

Is the lemon important?

What will happen if …?

The wheel on the motor is turning quite quickly.

motor

What makes this work?

wires

electrodes

lemon

Why …?

How …?

What happens if we use different fruits?

Which …?

When …?

Discuss

▶ What other **questions** can you ask about what is going on?

Electricity from a lemon

Which part of the lemon is needed to make electricity? Before you can find the answer to this **question**, you will need to ask other **questions**.

Plan

Find out which part of the lemon is used to make electricity. Use the questions below to help you.

◆ Does the motor turn when the electrodes are in the lemon skin?

◆ Does the motor turn when the electrodes are in the juice?

Record

▶ Make a record of what you did.
▶ Record the answer to the **question** 'Which part of the lemon is needed to make electricity?'

Electricity from other juices

In the investigation you have just done, you were given some **questions** to help you. Now you are going to try asking your own **questions**. One **question** you could ask is: 'Can you produce electricity using other juices?'

Discuss

▶ In your group, discuss this **question**.
▶ What do you think the answer is?
▶ What **questions** can you ask to find out more?
  Here are some examples:
  Will it work with vinegar?
  Will it work with water?

Plan

Find out if electricity can be produced using other juices.
◆ What **questions** do you need to ask?

Plan

Read the **questions** below.

◆ Is the distance between the electrodes important?
◆ Is the size of the electrodes important?
◆ Does it matter which way round you connect the motor?
◆ Does it work if the electrodes are the same?

Choose one of the **questions** and find out the answer to it. Ask other **questions** to help you find out more.

Record

▶ Make a record of what you did.
▶ Record your group's answer to the **question** you chose.
▶ Record the **questions** that your group found useful.
▶ Make a list of other **questions** you could ask that could help you find out more about the lemon and electricity.

Be scientific
—some useful words

accurate	evaluate	original
apply	exact	pattern
apparatus	experiment	persevere
assess	explain	physics
astronomy	explore	plan
attitude	fact	precise
belief	find out	predict
biology	forensic	present
book	help	process
change	honest	problem solving
chemistry	geology	question
checking	hypothesis	read
civilization	idea	record
classify	independence	relationships
communicate	infer	repeat
compare	information	research
computer	interact	responsibility
conclusion	interpret	self-criticism
control	invention	science
constant	investigate	scientific
cooperation	know	scientist
culture	listen	skill
curiosity	logic	standard
creative	manipulate	technology
critical	measure	theory
data	method	thinking
decide	mistake	truth
discuss	model	unbiased
encyclopaedia	natural	understanding
engineer	observe	universal
enquire	open-minded	useful
error	opinion	variable

Air

Contents

Air pressure	2.1
Birds	2.2
Boomerangs	2.3
Bubbles full of air	2.4
Falling through the air	2.5
Fire and safety	2.6
Flying things	2.7
Gases in the air	2.8
Ideas about burning	2.9
Jets	2.10
Sulphur dioxide	2.11
Using air movement	2.12
Water in the air	2.13
Weather	2.14
Why we need air	2.15
Air – some useful words	2.16

ymbols you will find:

These are things you should try to do.
These are extra things to do if you have time.
These are questions to think about when you are planning practical work.
When you see this symbol you need to take extra care.

is theme contains 15 spreads hich can be worked through in y order.

Theme 2

Air pressure

There are several kilometres of air above the Earth. The weight of this air presses on everything. This is called 'air pressure'.

Follow the plan

Here are four activities which show some of the effects of air pressure. You can do them in any order. Notice what happens in each case. You will be making **observations**.

⚠️ Gently push air from the syringe into the bottle.

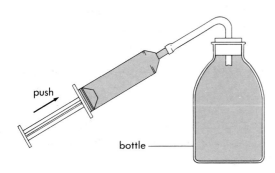

push

bottle

◆ What happens to the stopper?

⚠️ Only do this *over a sink!* Press the card on top of the cup.
Hold the cup in place and quickly turn it upside down.

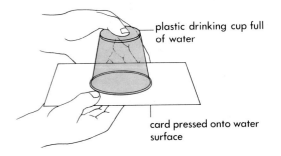

plastic drinking cup full of water

card pressed onto water surface

◆ What happens when you let go of the card?

Push the suction pad firmly onto the bench.

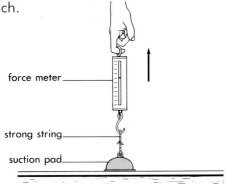

force meter

strong string

suction pad

◆ How much force is needed to pull the pad off the bench? (⚠️ Be careful – it may come away suddenly!)

Disinfect the ends of the tubes before you use them.
Suck some air out of the bottle using tube B.

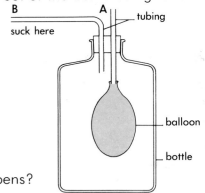

B   A

tubing

suck here

balloon

bottle

◆ What happens?
◆ What happens if you blow down tube A?

Discuss

▶ Do the exercise on Cut Out AR1 (part 1).

Record

▶ Keep a record of what you have done and what you have found out. Use Cut Out AR1 to help you.

Follow the plan

There are many different ways of measuring air pressure. One way is to use a Bourdon gauge which works like a party squeaker.

Disinfect the end of the squeaker before you use it.
Blow down the squeaker until it half unwinds.
Blow down it again until it fully unwinds.

◆ Does the feather uncurl clockwise or anti-clockwise?

The inside of the Bourdon gauge is metal and only moves slightly.

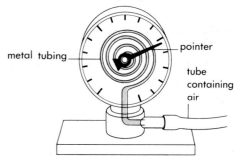

◆ Will the pointer turn clockwise or anti-clockwise when the air pressure is increased?

▶ Use your gauge to measure some air or gas pressures. Here are some ideas: the pressure needed to blow up a balloon; the gas pressure from your lungs; the air pressure from a bicycle pump.

Record

▶ Draw some diagrams to show how the squeaker moves.
▶ Describe how you think the air pressure moves the squeaker. You are making an **inference**.

▶ Make a list of the differences between your Bourdon gauge and the one in the diagram. You will have to make some careful **observations**.

Air pressure and the weather

People studying the weather need to know about air pressure.
Air moves from areas of high pressure to areas of low pressure. This movement is called 'wind'.

Discuss

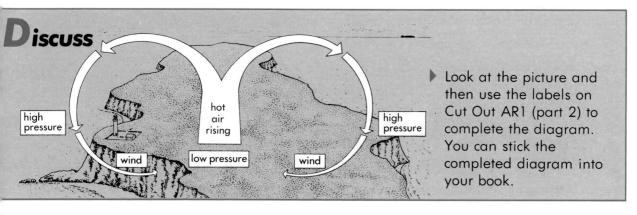

▶ Look at the picture and then use the labels on Cut Out AR1 (part 2) to complete the diagram. You can stick the completed diagram into your book.

Birds

Discuss

▶ Think of ten examples of animals which can fly through the air.
▶ Sort them into groups. This is your **classification**.

Most birds can fly through the air. They have different wing shapes which allow them to move through the air in different ways. They may dive, flap, glide or soar. The size and shape of birds' wings shows us something about the way they fly. Birds with large wings may fly for long periods. Birds with short wings may not fly very much.

You can also tell something about what different types of birds eat and where they live by looking at their beaks and feet. The things you notice about birds are your **observations**.

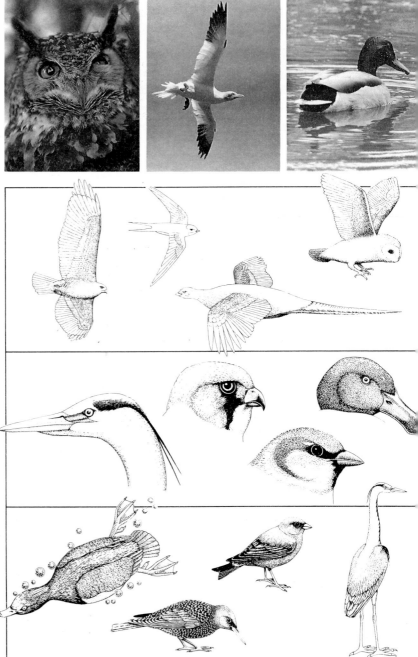

Discuss

▶ Do the exercise on Cut Out AR2.

Discuss

Imagine that people on an expedition have just discovered a bird called the 'gwosal'. This bird was not known before.

First reports say it is a fairly large bird with very small wings, a medium-sized, hooked beak, very large eyes, and long legs with webbed feet.
▶ Suggest where it lives, how it moves, and what it eats.

Observing birds gives you lots of information about them. When this information is sorted out, you can use it to identify a particular bird.

On this page are some pictures of birds, together with some more observations. The observations have been sorted out in a way that should make it easier to work out which bird is which. The observations have been **classified** to make a key.

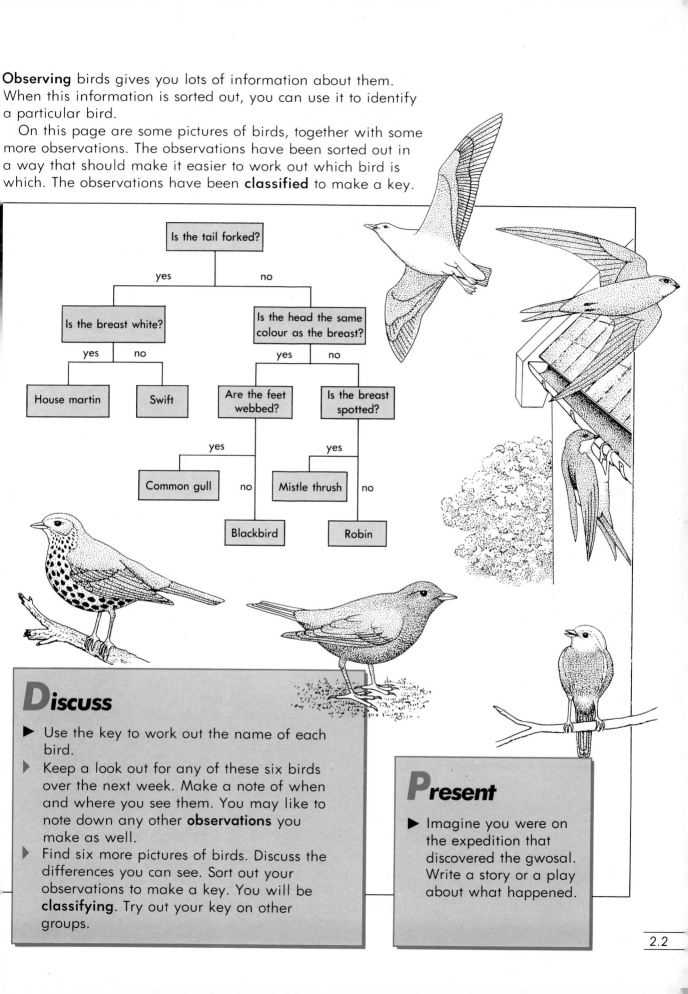

Is the tail forked?

yes — Is the breast white?
   yes — House martin
   no — Swift

no — Is the head the same colour as the breast?
   yes — Are the feet webbed?
      yes — Common gull
      no — Blackbird
   no — Is the breast spotted?
      yes — Mistle thrush
      no — Robin

Discuss

▶ Use the key to work out the name of each bird.

▶ Keep a look out for any of these six birds over the next week. Make a note of when and where you see them. You may like to note down any other **observations** you make as well.

▶ Find six more pictures of birds. Discuss the differences you can see. Sort out your observations to make a key. You will be **classifying**. Try out your key on other groups.

Present

▶ Imagine you were on the expedition that discovered the gwosal. Write a story or a play about what happened.

Boomerangs

Boomerangs are an interesting type of flying object. They are similar to the wing designs in spread 2.5. However, they are designed not to hover in the air, but to spin through it.

When a boomerang is thrown it follows a curved path through the air as it spins. With enough space, a boomerang may curve around and return to you.

In this activity you will find out about two different designs of boomerang. You will **investigate** the ways in which they fly.

Discuss

▶ What do you think boomerangs could be used for?
▶ What do you think makes the best boomerang?

Plan

There are two designs of boomerang on Cut Out AR3. One is drawn in solid lines and one is drawn in dotted lines. Trace these onto stiff card and try them out. You can also try different sizes and different types of material.

⚠ Make sure you *do not* flick the boomerangs towards anyone's face.

Launching method 1

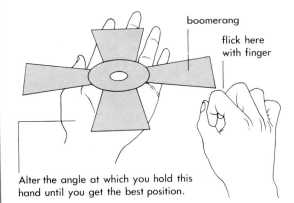

boomerang

flick here with finger

Alter the angle at which you hold this hand until you get the best position.

Launching method 2

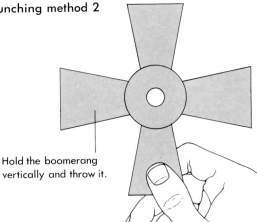

Hold the boomerang vertically and throw it.

◆ How does the launching method you use make a difference to the way the boomerang flies?
◆ Does the size of the boomerang make a difference?
◆ How does the type of material you use affect the boomerang?

Record

▶ Make some drawings to show the shape of the flight path for each of your boomerangs.

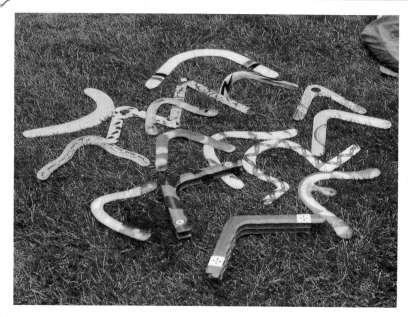

Boomerangs which return to the thrower are now made all over the world, although they are often thought of as Australian. Look at the shapes of these boomerangs. Some have two or three wings. Others have weights at their tips.

Plan

Try this **investigation**. Add small weights to the tips of your card boomerangs to find out what effect they have.

Present

▶ Make a poster to display your boomerangs. Put on to it some information about each one. How well does each one fly?

Boomerangs were probably developed from throw-sticks which were designed to fly in a straight line. The picture shows an ancient Egyptian nobleman throwing throw-sticks into a flock of waterbirds. It was painted in about 1600 BC.

Discuss

▶ If you look carefully you can see some throw-sticks in the flock. What effect have they had?
▶ How could throw-sticks be used today?
▶ In what sort of place could they be used?
You are making some **inferences** about throw-sticks.

Bubbles full of air

Plan

Use the prepared solution to blow some bubbles. Find out about bubbles and how to make them. The questions below give you some ideas to start your **investigation**.

⚠ Make sure you keep away from electricity and work over a sink. Always wear eye protection.

◆ How can you measure the size of your bubbles?

◆ What are their shapes and colours?

◆ How much of the solution do you use to make 20 bubbles?

◆ What is the best sort of blow to use?

Try using a polystyrene cup with a hole in the bottom to blow bubbles.

▶ Try using other things to make better bubbles.

Discuss

Use your **observations** to discuss the following questions.
▶ What do you think is inside the bubbles?
▶ What do you think causes bubbles to change their shape?
You have made some **inferences** about bubbles.

▶ What does your group think of this idea:

'A bubble's skin is always moving. It is pushed around by the particles of air moving inside it'.

This is a **hypothesis**.

Record

▶ Draw a coloured picture of a large bubble.
▶ Make a table of all the different types of bubbles you can think of. Use the headings 'size','made of', and 'filled with'.
▶ Describe what you think is happening inside a

bubble. This will be your **hypothesis**. Try drawing a model.
▶ Find some pictures of bubbles in different places and add them to your table. Use the library to help you carry out this **investigation**.

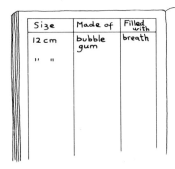

Size	Made of	Filled with
12 cm	bubble gum	breath
" "		

Plan

Find out whether the size of a bubble depends on the concentration of your prepared solution. Use the hints below to help you plan your **investigation**.

Find out what is in the prepared solution.

Make some solutions of your own.

Decide what to look for. You will need to make some useful **observations**. Decide what instruments you will need to help you measure your observations.

Decide how to record your observations.

◆ Which solution gives you the biggest bubble?

Plan

Find out whether the size of the bubbles depends on the size of the former.

Use your 'best' solution to blow bubbles in this **investigation**.

Change the size of the former.

Use different sized polystyrene cups.

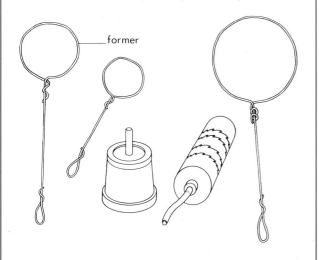

former

▶ Ask your teacher to show you how bubbles can be filled with different gases.

Discuss

▶ How can you change the size of the bubbles?
▶ Look at the picture closely. It shows an idea for a bubble roundabout. Can you suggest how it might work? You are making an **inference**.
▶ You may like to try out this 'bubble roundabout' or design one of your own.

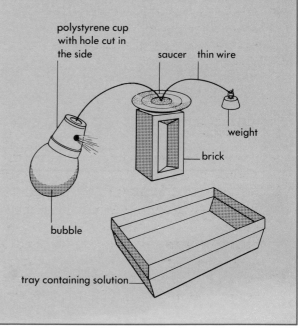

polystyrene cup with hole cut in the side

saucer   thin wire

weight

brick

bubble

tray containing solution

Falling through the air

In this activity you will find out about different designs of parachute. You will do some **investigations**.

Discuss

▶ Look at the photograph. What do you think the parachute is used for? This is your **inference**.
▶ How can you make a parachute? What materials will be best?
▶ Will the size of the material make a difference?
▶ Does the shape matter? (Some parachutes have holes!)
▶ Will the way you join the materials together make a difference? You are making some **predictions**.

Plan

Here is one design for a parachute (you may like to try others). Even with this design there are many parts that you can easily change. Decide what you must do to find out more about parachutes and how you will do a fair test.

Cut out a circle of material about 20 cm across.

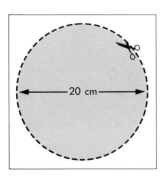

Cut some 30 cm lengths of cotton. Join one end of each to the circle at regular intervals.

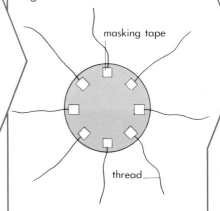

Join together the free ends of the cotton and tie on a load such as a paper clip.

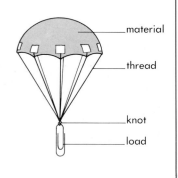

Record

▶ Write a report to show what you have done.
▶ Record which parachute gave the best result.

Present

▶ Make a poster showing the parachutes you made and how you tested them.

Some plant seeds have wings which slow their fall through the air. A seed will have a better chance of being blown away from its parent tree if it can stay in the air for a long time. A seed growing away from its parent will have more chance of finding the room and light that it needs to develop.

Plan

Find out about other wing designs. Decide on a fair test to compare them. You will be doing an **investigation**. Here is one simple design to start you off.

Mark out this shape onto a piece of paper.

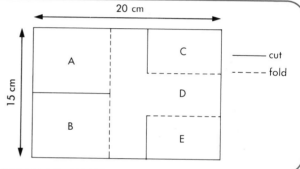

Cut it out carefully.

▶ Try to make the wing spin in the opposite direction.

Fold C and E over D and fix with a paper clip.
Fold A and B in opposite directions.

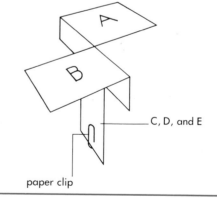

▶ Try different lengths of wing, different materials, and different numbers of paper clips.

Record

▶ Write a report on what you have done.

▶ Record which design was best. This is your **evaluation**.

Fire and safety

Discuss

▶ How could you help to prevent a fire starting in your home or school?
▶ If a fire did start, how could you help to stop it from spreading?

The fire extinguisher

A fire extinguisher is one device which can be used to control a fire. Here are some facts which are used to design the foam fire extinguisher.

a) When acid is mixed with sodium hydrogen carbonate, it produces carbon dioxide gas.

b) When gas is produced in washing-up liquid it foams.

c) Carbon dioxide foam does not let things burn.

Follow the plan

Make a fire extinguisher, then try it out on a small fire. For safety this must be done in a sink, but remember to remove the burned paper afterwards (or you will block the sink).

Mix several spatulas of sodium hydrogen carbonate with some washing up liquid in a beaker of water.
Pour the mixture into a plastic wash bottle.

Tie a string around a small test tube. Pour a little dilute acid into the test tube and lower it into the wash bottle.

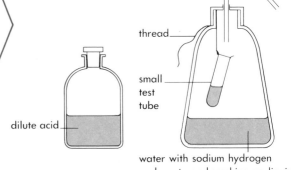

thread

small test tube

dilute acid

water with sodium hydrogen carbonate and washing up liquid

Record

▶ Describe in your own words how you set up your extinguisher.
▶ In your description, explain where facts (a), (b), and (c) are **applied**.
▶ How well did your extinguisher work? You are **evaluating** your extinguisher.

Put the top back on the wash bottle. It should produce foam when you shake it and the acid touches the mixture.

⚠ Use your fire extinguisher to put out a small fire of scrap paper.

The fire alarm

A fire alarm can detect a fire and warn people to take action.
These two facts can be used to design a fire alarm.

d) Different types of metal expand by different amounts when they are heated.

e) Metals conduct electricity.

The information is **applied**.

Follow the plan

Two pieces of metal joined together are a 'bimetallic strip'.
Follow the instructions to make your fire alarm.

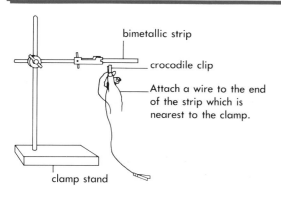

bimetallic strip

crocodile clip

Attach a wire to the end of the strip which is nearest to the clamp.

clamp stand

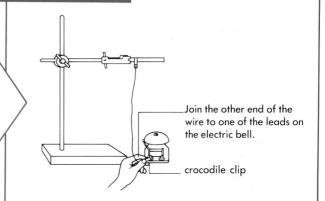

Join the other end of the wire to one of the leads on the electric bell.

crocodile clip

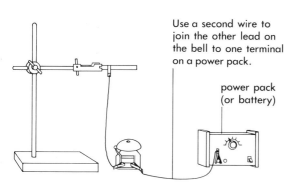

Use a second wire to join the other lead on the bell to one terminal on a power pack.

power pack (or battery)

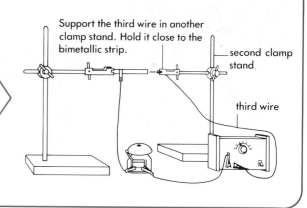

Support the third wire in another clamp stand. Hold it close to the bimetallic strip.

second clamp stand

third wire

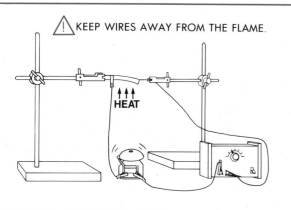

⚠ KEEP WIRES AWAY FROM THE FLAME.

HEAT

Record

▶ Draw diagrams to show how you set up your alarm.
▶ Mark on your diagrams where you have used facts (d) and (e). You have **applied** this information.
▶ **Evaluate** your alarm.

Flying things

Fay had been trying to drop the wrapper from a bar of chocolate into the waste bin, but the paper had missed its target three times in a row! Finally, she crumpled the wrapper into a ball. This time it fell straight into the bin. She decided to get her group to find out whether some shapes are easier to aim than others. This is the **investigation** they did.

First they dropped a paper shape towards a target ten times.

Then they made different shapes and tried dropping them in the same way.

Finally they used different types of paper to make their shapes and tested them too.

Plan

Now plan an investigation like the one Fay's group did. You can use any shapes you like, but here are two ideas to start you off.

A paper star

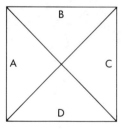

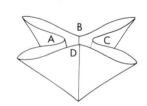

Fold a paper square along its diagonals. Unfold it into a square again.

Fold A, B, C, and D into the centre and fasten them together.

A paper pyramid

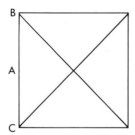

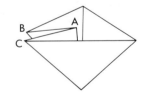

Fold a paper square along its diagonals. Unfold it into a square again.

Fold A into the centre and fasten B to C.

Record

▶ Record your results in a table rather like this one. These are your **observations**. (How will you decide when you have a 'near miss'?)

Shape	Type of paper	Hit	Near miss	Way off
Flat	Tissue	3	6	1
Flat	Scrap	0	1	9
Ball	Scrap	2	4	4
Star	Scrap	6	3	1

Fay's group then used their results to design some paper darts. They wanted their darts to be accurate (hit a target) and to go as far as possible as well.

Plan

Use your results to design and make some paper darts that will travel a long way and land near a target. You will be **applying** the information you have already gathered. How far away you put the target will depend on whether you are testing your darts indoors or outdoors.

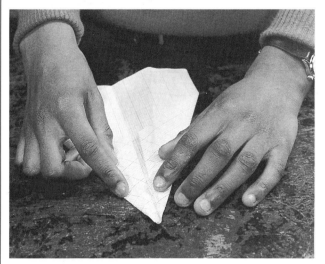

◆ Do different types of paper make a difference to the way your darts fly? How will you measure your **observations**?

◆ Are paper darts that work well *outdoors* different in design from those which work well *indoors*?

Plan

Suggest ways of changing your dart so it will stay in the air for as long as possible. You are **predicting**.
▶ Test out your ideas. You will be doing an **experiment**.

Present

▶ Make a display of your darts giving details of the performance of each one. This is your **evaluation**.

Gases in the air

Caroline's group had been learning about the gases in the air. They had found out that the air is a mixture of gases. Three of these gases are oxygen, nitrogen, and carbon dioxide.

The group started to argue about the bubbles in lemonade. They all agreed that the bubbles contained a gas, but Caroline thought the gas was carbon dioxide while the others thought it was nitrogen.

Discuss

▶ Do you think Caroline is right or wrong?
▶ How could you find out?

Follow the plan

Here are four tests which you can carry out on oxygen, nitrogen, and carbon dioxide (12 tests altogether). You can do them in any order. You will need to use a fresh test tube of gas for each test. Make sure you do not remove the bung from a test tube until you are ready to carry out a test.

Lighted splint test

Light a splint and put it into the test tube.

◆ What happens?

Glowing splint test

Light a splint and then blow it out so that only the tip is glowing. Put the glowing splint into the test tube.

◆ What happens?

Indicator test

Put a little water into the tube. Shake the tube, then add a few drops of indicator solution. Shake again.

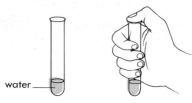

◆ What happens to the indicator?

Lime water test

Put a few drops of lime water into the test tube. Shake the tube.

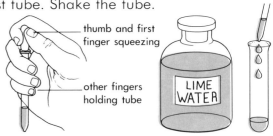

◆ What happens to the lime water?

Record

▶ Make a table to show your results. Your results are your **observations**.

Discuss

Look back at Caroline's group's ideas and the table you have just made. The group decide to try the gas tests on the lemonade bubbles.

▶ What do you think will happen with the different gas tests if Caroline is right? These are your **predictions**.

▶ What do you think will happen with the gas tests if Caroline is wrong and the rest of the group is right? You are now making more **predictions**.

▶ Check with your teacher that your predictions are correct.

Plan

You can use the predictions you have made to see if Caroline was right. You will need to collect the lemonade gas to carry out your **experiment**.

Shake up some lemonade in a test tube. Quickly use the delivery tube to collect the gas. To do this you will need to put the end of the delivery tube at the bottom of a clean test tube.

Collect a fresh sample of the gas before doing each of the four tests.

When you are doing the lime water test, it may be easier to bubble the lemonade gas through lime water that is already in the test tube.

Discuss

▶ What do you think the bubbles contain now? You have **interpreted** your results.

▶ Does this agree with what you thought earlier?

Record

▶ Describe how you carried out your experiment.

Discuss

▶ What do you think happens when something burns?

These cartoons follow the development of some ideas about burning.

The time is the 1700s. A scientist is thinking about fire.

Time moves on to 1774. Joseph Priestley is working in his laboratory.

Meanwhile, somewhere in France...

2.9

Discuss

► Re-read the cartoons. Decide whether the statements in the bubbles are

  hypotheses   **observations**
  inferences   **predictions**.

► How have your ideas about burning changed?

Record

► Make a list of each type of statement above.

► Find out whether Madame Lavoisier's last prediction came true.

► Write a story about the Lavoisiers.

Jets

Danny and Vida were looking at the fountain the council had just built.

'It's not very good', said Vida.

'If they could afford to make the water go faster, it would go higher and look better', commented Danny.

'They could get it to go higher just by making the hole smaller', replied Vida.

Discuss

Danny and Vida each have an idea about how to make the fountain higher.

▶ Pick out their ideas. These are their **hypotheses**.

▶ What are your group's ideas about how to make the fountain higher? These are your **hypotheses**.

Plan

Now use this method to test Danny's and Vida's hypotheses.
This will be your **experiment**.

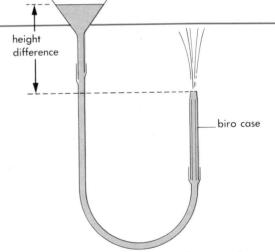

height difference

biro case

Raise the funnel above the jet. The higher the water level in the funnel, the faster the water will go through the jet.

◆ What happens when you change the height difference?

◆ What happens when you change the size of the hole?
You have made some **observations**.

▶ Test your group's hypotheses.

Record

▶ Record Danny's and Vida's hypotheses?

▶ Use diagrams to show how you tested the hypotheses.

▶ Record whether or not you agree with them.

▶ Jets of liquid can be very useful. Make a list of places and situations where you have seen jets of liquid being used.

When Vida's group had done the water jet activity, one of them said 'I bet you get jets of gas in the same way, but they're more difficult to see'. He was making a **prediction**.

Plan

They used a Bunsen burner and a balloon to test the prediction. They carried out some **experiments**. Try some similar experiments in your own group. You will need to make some **observations** as you go along.

Use a Bunsen burner with the barrel unscrewed and removed. Turn the burner off as soon as you have finished.

⚠️What happens to the size of the flame when you turn up the gas tap?

Discuss

▶ In what way does the jet move the balloon?
▶ Could the gas jet move the burner?

◆ How can you show there is something coming out of the balloon?
◆ What happens if you alter the size of the opening?
◆ What happens when you let go of the balloon?

Record

▶ Write down the prediction you have tested.
▶ Draw a diagram for each experiment showing how it tests the prediction.
▶ Record whether you agree or disagree with the prediction.

Sulphur dioxide

When something is not clean or pure, it may be 'polluted'. Sulphur dioxide is a gas that pollutes the air. It can come from factories or cars, or anything that burns coal or oil. Volcanoes can also produce sulphur dioxide when they erupt.

Sulphur dioxide and plants

Follow the plan

You are going to find out the effect of sulphur dioxide on plants. You will use a solution of sodium metabisulphite to get some sulphur dioxide. You will need to leave this **investigation** set up for at least a week.

Put equal amounts of cotton wool into two labelled beakers.

Soak the cotton wool in A with water and the cotton wool in B with sodium metabisulphite solution. Use the same amount for each.

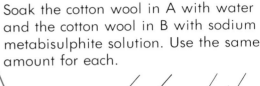
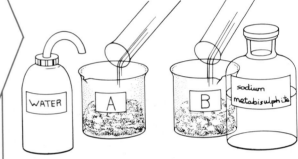

Put 20 cress seeds in each beaker and seal the beakers with cling film.

◆ What happens after a week?

Record

▶ Draw diagrams to show what you have done.

▶ Write a report to describe what happened.

Discuss

▶ Why was it important to use the same amounts of:
   a) water and sodium metabisulphite
   b) cotton wool
   c) cress seeds in each beaker?

Gregor's group did this investigation.

At the end of it they said 'This does not show the effect of sulphur dioxide gas on the seeds, it shows the effect of sodium metabisulphite solution'. They were **evaluating** their investigation.

▶ Is this a fair criticism? Can you improve the investigation to take this criticism into account?

Sulphur dioxide and buildings

Acid rain is a name given to rain water which has sulphur dioxide dissolved in it.

Kumud's group had been doing some work on acid rain. They had found out that acids dissolve some substances. They had also noticed that the marble statues in the park were wearing away. They thought that acid rain might be damaging the statues. This was their **inference**.

They decided to test their ideas. They poured 'acid rain' (sulphur dioxide and water) onto a marble chip. This was their **experiment**.

'There you are', they said, when they saw the result. 'Ordinary rain wouldn't do that'.

Plan

Try their experiment yourselves.

Discuss

▶ Do you think your results support the group's ideas?
▶ Is it a fair test? **Evaluate** your experiment.
▶ How could you improve the experiment? Could you make the testing more fair?

Record

▶ Write down the inference you were testing.
▶ Record what happened when you did the test. The things you noticed are your **observations**.
▶ Record your ideas about the fairness of the test.

Windmills

Moving air is a good source of energy. Wind is easily available and does not cause pollution.

One way of getting energy from the wind is to use a windmill. Windmills were invented in Persia (modern-day Iran) over a thousand years ago. Since then they have been used for many different jobs.

Two major uses of windmills have been to grind corn into flour and to drain water from low lying land. Recently, people have been looking at the possibility of using windmills to generate electricity.

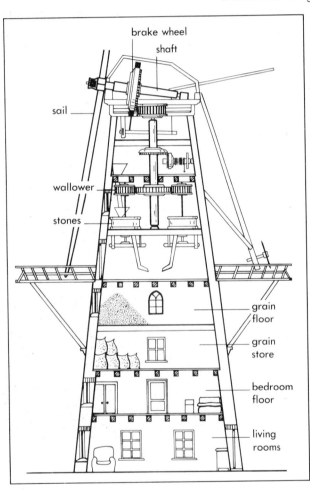

Follow the plan

You can make your own windmill. You will need a square of paper, some way of fastening the paper (clips, glue or sellotape), and something to pin the sails on (e.g. a straw).

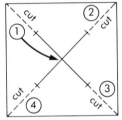

Cut along each line as far as A (half way to the centre).

Now take points 1, 2, 3, and 4 to the centre and fasten them with a pin.

Fix the pin onto a straw or thin piece of wood so that the sails can rotate when you blow on them.

▶ Try to improve on this design.

Discuss

▶ Arrange these sentences in an order which best describes how the mill works.

The wallower turns the stones.

The moving sails turn the shaft, which turns the brake wheel.

The sails are turned by the wind.

The stones grind the corn.

The brake wheel turns the wallower through a gearing system.

Sailing ships

Another way in which the power of the wind has been used is in sailing. Ships and boats have been making use of wind energy for even longer than windmills.

Discuss

▶ Look at these statements and photographs.

▶ Decide which statement goes best with each of the photos.

▶ Decide whether each statement is an advantage or a disadvantage for a sailing ship.

▶ Are the advantages or disadvantages very important, quite important, or not important at all? You will be making **inferences**.

A sailing ship uses simple technology so it is quite easy to repair.

Handling a large sailing ship is much more complicated than using an engine and so requires greater skill.

Masts and ropes clutter up deck and cargo space.

Sailing ships can only be steered in certain directions, depending on the direction of the wind.

Sailing ships need a large crew to work all the sails.

The wind is free.

The wind does not cause pollution.

Wind may not blow for days, or may vary greatly in strength. It is hard to run a regular service using wind power.

Record

▶ Record your results in a table headed 'Advantages and disadvantages of wind power'.

▶ Try to think of some other advantages or disadvantages to add to your table.

Water in the air

Air usually contains water. The amount of water in the air is called its 'humidity'.

Discuss

We sometimes say that the weather is 'humid'.

▶ What does this mean?
▶ Are there any other ways of telling it is humid?

Plan

Find out what effect water has on cobalt chloride paper (blue) and copper sulphate powder (white). You will be doing an **investigation**. The substances will probably be stored ready for use in a desiccator. Inside a desiccator the air is kept very dry.

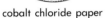

cobalt chloride paper

copper sulphate powder

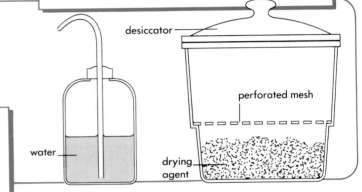

desiccator

perforated mesh

water

drying agent

Record

▶ Make a 'before and after' table to show your **observations**.

Plan

Ali's group did this activity. They came up with this idea. '*Any liquid will change the colour of blue cobalt chloride and white copper sulphate.*' This was their **hypothesis**.

Plan and carry out a series of ways to test their idea. You will be **experimenting**.

Check your results before going on to the next section.

Plan

The group also wanted to see if water in the air had the same effect on the two substances as liquid water. They carried out this **investigation**.

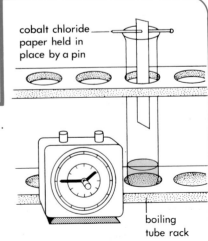

cobalt chloride paper held in place by a pin

boiling tube rack

Shake the boiling tube and water before putting the paper in. Make certain that the paper does not touch the liquid or the sides of the tube.

◆ What happens to the cobalt chloride paper? What **observations** can you make?
◆ They could not think how to test copper sulphate powder in the same way. Can you?

Testing humidity

Sonia's group had this idea. 'The more water there is in the air, the quicker cobalt chloride paper changes colour!' This was their **hypothesis**. They decided to use their idea to compare the humidity of different classrooms. This is how they did their **investigation**.

They used six pieces of blue cobalt chloride paper from the desiccator and tested six classrooms in turn. In each room they timed how long it was before the colour of the paper changed. Below you can see what they did and the results they got.

Room number	127	61	31a	42	11	219
Time for colour to change (mins)	10	9	11	12	8	14

Discuss

▶ According to their results, which room was most humid?

Plan

Carry out an **investigation** in your own group. Find out how the humidity of the air varies in your school.

Chemicals which make the air less humid

We need dry air to store cobalt chloride paper or white copper sulphate powder. One way of drying the air is to use a desiccator. This is a large, airtight jar with a special compartment for a 'drying agent'. A drying agent is a chemical which absorbs water from the air. Calcium chloride is a common drying agent.

Plan

Weigh some calcium chloride in a dish. Leave the dish on a shelf for a week.
◆ What happened to the weight of the dish of calcium chloride? This is your **observation**.

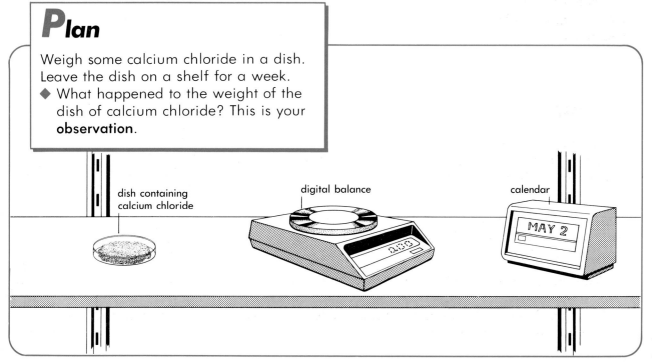

dish containing calcium chloride

digital balance

calendar

MAY 2

'Red sky at night – shepherds delight.
Red sky in the morning – shepherds warning.'

You may have heard this saying before. It is an old rural way of telling what the weather will be like. The people who made it up had noticed a pattern.

a) Good weather follows sunsets that leave a red glow in the sky.

b) Poor weather follows sunrises that make the sky glow red.

These were their **observations**. They did not try to explain them. But they used their observations to forecast the weather, or make **predictions**.

Nowadays, meteorologists (people who study the weather) not only look for patterns but also try to suggest explanations for the things they notice. The explanations they make are their **inferences**. These explanations make it easier to forecast, or **predict**, the weather. The table shows some observations of weather conditions made by meteorologists, together with some of the inferences and predictions they made.

What they noticed (their **observations**)	How they explained it (their **inferences**)	What they thought would happen (their **predictions**)
Thin, wispy clouds high in the sky. Clear, sunny weather.	These clouds are too high to bring bad weather.	If the clouds stayed the same the weather would remain clear and sunny.
Large dark clouds. Rain had previously fallen from clouds like these.	There is a lot of water in these clouds.	Rain or hail will fall from these clouds.
A bright flash of lightning, followed by thunder.	The lightning caused the thunder.	If there is another flash of lightning there will be more thunder.

Record

▶ Sort out the sentences on Cut Out AR4 (part 1) to make three more observations/inferences/predictions like the ones above.

Windy weather

One thing that is very important for meteorologists to know is the speed of the wind. Knowing the speed of the wind can help them to **predict** how quickly and when the weather will change. Windspeed can be described using the Beaufort Scale, which was originally designed for use at sea.

The Beaufort Scale

Number	Type	Speed (km/h)	What you would see. These are **observations**
0	calm	0–1	sea like a mirror
1	light air	1–5	sea with ripples
2	slight breeze	6–11	small waves, crests do not break
3	gentle breeze	12–19	wave crests begin to break
4	moderate breeze	20–28	frequent white horses (foaming wave crests)
5	fresh breeze	29–38	moderate waves, many white horses, some spray
6	strong breeze	39–49	large waves, crests of waves break with patches of foam
7	moderate gale	50–61	sea begins to tower, foam blown by wind
8	gale	62–74	high, long waves
9	strong gale	75–88	mountainous waves, spray affects visibility
10	whole gale	89–102	mountainous waves, sea white with foam
11	storm	103–117	exceptionally large waves, visibility much reduced by spray
12	hurricane	over 118	air filled with foam and spray, sea completely white, no distant objects can be seen

Discuss

▶ On Cut Out AR4 (part 2) are some more statements about the Beaufort Scale. They describe what you would notice on land during each type of wind, so they are **observations**. In your group, decide on an order from 0 to 12.

Record

▶ Describe the winds you think are blowing in the photographs.
▶ Write a story about being caught in a sailing boat when the weather suddenly changed from calm to storm.

How does air get into the lungs?

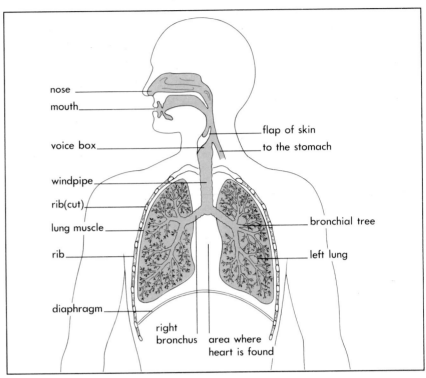

- nose
- mouth
- voice box
- windpipe
- rib(cut)
- lung muscle
- rib
- diaphragm
- flap of skin
- to the stomach
- bronchial tree
- left lung
- right bronchus
- area where heart is found

Breathing is the most important thing that we do. We do it so regularly that normally we do not even think about it.

Discuss

▶ Why do you think that breathing is so important? You may be able to make some **inferences** about breathing.

To keep our bodies going we need a constant supply of energy. In the air there is a gas which will release the energy from our food. As we breathe we get this gas from the air through our lungs.

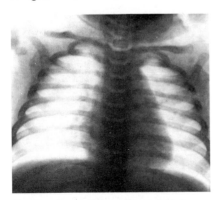

This X-ray was taken after a harmless chemical had been breathed into the lung. The white parts show the air spaces in the lung.

Look at the two diagrams. The first shows the breathing system inside your body. The ribs and diaphragm make an airtight cover all the way round the lungs, broken only where the windpipe enters. The second diagram shows a model of this system. By pulling down the rubber sheet you can make the balloons fill up.

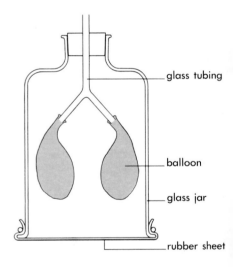

- glass tubing
- balloon
- glass jar
- rubber sheet

Discuss

▶ There are four labelled parts in the model. Which parts of the real system do they represent? You are **interpreting** the model.
▶ Which of the parts work in the same way? Which work differently?
▶ How does the movement of the rubber sheet make the balloons blow up? You are making an **inference**.

What gases are used by your body?

Some doctors were finding out about breathing. They did the following **investigation**. They took samples of air breathed out from a group of volunteers. The results are shown in Graph 1.

They found that the air breathed in had more oxygen than the air breathed out. However, there was less carbon dioxide in the air breathed in than in the air breathed out. The nitrogen level hardly changed at all.

They **inferred** that our bodies take oxygen from the air and put carbon dioxide into it.

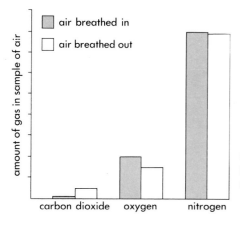

Graph 1

Graph showing the changes between air breathed in and air breathed out.

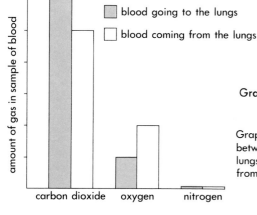

Graph 2

Graph showing the changes between blood going to the lungs and blood coming from the lungs.

Record

The doctors did a further **investigation**, taking blood samples. The results are shown in Graph 2.
▶ Write two paragraphs, like the ones above, explaining these results. Try to suggest a **hypothesis** to explain what gases are used by your body.

Smoking and lungs

The lungs are very delicate and smoke from cigarettes, cigars, and pipes can damage them in a number of ways.

Discuss

▶ Find out what smoking does to :
   a) lung tissue
   b) the mouth
   c) the blood

▶ How do people try to stop others smoking?

▶ How do people try to encourage smoking?

Present

▶ Organize a debate on smoking. Here are some ideas to help you.
   a) Find out some reasons people give for smoking. What do you think of these?
   b) Collect together a variety of anti–smoking material. Which do you think is most effective? You are **evaluating** the materials.

Air—some useful words

aeration

aerodynamic

aeroplane

air conditioner

anemometer

anticyclone

argon

atmosphere

aviation

barometer

birds

blow

blue

breathing

breeze

bubbles

carbon dioxide

cirrus

climate

cloud

cool

cumulus

cyclone

deflate

doldrums

draught

drying

dust

evaporate

fan

fog

gas

gasp

heater

hot

humidifier

inflate

meteorology

millibar

mist

neon

nitrogen

oxygen

ozone

plants

pneumatic

pressure

respire

seeds

suck

thin

ventilate

warm

water vapour

wind

Chemicals
Contents

Chemicals from bees	3.1
Chemicals in our food	3.2
Dissolving chemicals	3.3
Distilling salty water	3.4
Dyes	3.5
Green dye from leaves	3.6
Heating materials	3.7
Indicators	3.8
Investigating chemical changes	3.9
A mystery illness	3.10
Pesticides	3.11
Salt	3.12
Separating chemicals	3.13
Stomach acid	3.14
Using chemicals safely	3.15
Chemicals — some useful words	3.16

Symbols you will find:

▶ These are things you should try to do.

▸ These are extra things to do if you have time.

◆ These are questions to think about when you are planning practical work.

⚠ When you see this symbol you need to take extra care.

This theme contains 15 spreads which can be worked through in any order.

Theme 3

Chemicals from bees

Discuss

Discuss these questions before you read the information about bees.
► Where do bees live?
► Why do they visit flowers?
► What is honey made from?
► What is honey comb made from?

Bees

Bees are found in most parts of the world. Some bees live in 'colonies', or large groups. Others are 'solitary', or live alone.

Honey

To make honey, bees use the nectar from flowers or the juices from aphids. The bees suck up the nectar and mix it with some stomach juices and pollen. They carry this mixture back to the hive. This makes the honey that they store to use as food.

The hive

This is where the bees store food for the winter and rear their young , called 'larvae'. The honey is stored in the comb. The bees build the comb with wax which they make in their bodies.

Record

► Use Cut Out CH1 (part 1) to explain how bees make honey.

Beeswax and honey

Beekeepers provide hives for colonies of bees to live in. Beekeepers collect honey and beeswax from the hives. They use a honey spinner to separate the honey from the comb.

Record

► Use Cut Out CH1 (part 2) to describe how honey is separated from beeswax.

Different sorts of honey

Bees produce honey of different types depending on where they live and the nectar they use.

Record

Collect some different types of honey.

▶ Make a table showing where each honey comes from, what it is made of, its colour and any other information you can find out.
You are **interpreting**.

▶ Find out if other members of your class eat honey.

▶ Find out what they use the honey for.

Present

▶ Make a collection of honey jar labels. Do drawings if you cannot get the real labels.
▶ Display them on a large sheet.

Beeswax

The wax from the combs can be used in a number of ways. Some of these are shown here.

Record

▶ From the pictures record the different ways beeswax can be used.
▶ Decide what job it does in each case. You are **interpreting**.
▶ In each case find out the name of a chemical which could be used instead of beeswax.

Chemicals in our food

You probably eat some 'convenience' foods — food which you can eat without having to do much cooking. Most of these foods have chemicals added to them to make them last, to give them flavour, and to make them look good.

Discuss

Look at the lists below of ingredients for different sorts of tomato soup.
► Decide which of the ingredients are natural chemicals.
► Discuss your decisions with your teacher.
► Look at each list of ingredients and decide which ingredients are *necessary* for making soup.
► Decide which ingredients are added but are *not necessary*.

Ingredients for tomato soup — three examples

Instant cup of tomato soup

Sugar, tomato powder, modified starch, dried glucose syrup, salt, vegetable fat, whole milk powder, monosodium glutamate, acidity regulator E340, emulsifiers E471 and E472b, colours E124 and E102, malic acid, antioxidant E320.

Tinned tomato soup

Tomatoes, water, fresh milk, sugar, wheat flour, butter, vegetable oil, modified starch, cream, salt, dried skimmed milk, spices, citric acid.

Home-made tomato soup

600 g tomatoes, lemon, carrot, 25 g butter, 25 g flour, 600 cm^3 stock, bay leaf, 10 g sugar, pinch of nutmeg, 5 g salt, black pepper, 20 cm^3 cream.

Record

► Make a list of the chemicals given in all three recipes.
► Make a table showing how you decided to group the ingredients. Make two column headings for your table:

Necessary	Not necessary

and list the ingredients under the right heading. You will be **classifying** the ingredients.
► Make a list of any ingredients which you could not classify.

Discuss

► Think about how you could find out which ingredients are essential for making tomato soup. You may need to talk to your Home Economics teacher and make some soup.
► Not everyone makes home-made soup. Think of some reasons why people use tinned or packet soup instead.

Adding chemicals

Chemicals like salt, sugar, and citric acid have been added to foods for some years. Nowadays there are also many processed foods in our shops which have chemicals called 'additives' in them. There are six main sorts of additives. The table shows some information about each of them. It also gives the E numbers which are used instead of the long chemical names. You will see a list of ingredients and additives on most foods you buy.

	What the chemicals do	E Number
Colours	These make the food look more attractive to some people. Many colours are natural, some are artificial. It is mostly the artificial ones which have E numbers.	E100 – E180
Preservatives	These stop bacteria growing in food and turning it bad. Some have been known for a very long time, like salt and alcohol. The newer ones have E numbers.	E200 – E290
Antioxidants	Air by itself can spoil food. Butter goes rancid in air. These chemicals stop or slow down the reaction with oxygen.	E300 – E321
Emulsifiers	These chemicals stop separation of creamy liquids like mayonnaise which are made of oils and water.	E322 – E494
Sweeteners	These sweeten foods without using sugar.	E420 and E421
Modified starches	These thicken liquids like soups.	E1400 – E1442

Present

▶ Look closely at different packaged foods. There are some shown here. Choose one of these foods or one that you have found. Place the label in the middle of a large sheet of paper. Leave plenty of space around it.
▶ Use the information given in the table and add the correct facts to your poster. Design it so that anyone eating this food can find out exactly what they are getting. You will be **applying**.

Side effects

In Britain there is a law which says that processed foods must list all their ingredients. There are more than 450 chemicals used in foods in Britain. Over 400 of them usually have no bad effects. Some of the others cause side effects for some people. People may be 'allergic' to these chemicals. Some people think that everyone would be more healthy if they did not use additives at all. Others disagree.

Discuss

▶ Read Cut Out CH2. Divide up the ideas in your group and discuss each of them.

Present

▶ Organize a debate about whether food should contain additives. Use the ideas from Cut Out CH2 to help you.

Dissolving chemicals

Some substances seem to disappear in water.
They 'dissolve' in water.

Follow the plan

Find out what happens to salt and sand when you put them in water. You will be **investigating**.

Half fill two test tubes with water. Make sure the levels are the same. Put a spatula-full of salt in one and a spatula-full of clean sand in the other. Mark the liquid levels.

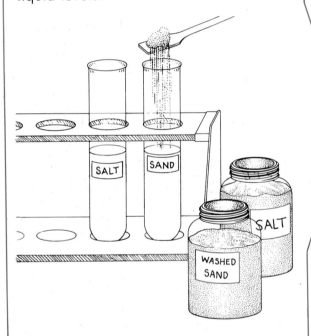

Discuss

▶ What chemicals do you know that dissolve in water?

Put a stopper in each tube then shake them carefully.

◆ Do the liquid levels change?
◆ What happens to the salt and sand?
◆ What do the tubes feel like if you put them against your skin?
◆ What other **observations** did you make?
▶ Try doing the investigation using other chemicals. Use copper turnings, sugar, small stones, or copper sulphate.
◆ Does using hot water change your results? Try hot water with each substance.

Record

▶ Look at your test tubes and write down what you think has happened to each of the chemicals. You will be **inferring**. Use the table to help you.

Your observation after shaking	Inference
I can still see *all* of the chemical.	None of the chemical has dissolved in water.
I can still see *some* of the chemical.	Some of the chemical has dissolved in water.
I cannot see *any* of the chemical.	All the chemical has dissolved in water.

Discuss

▶ What do you think happens to chemicals when they dissolve? This will be your **hypothesis**.

Solutions which are full

When you dissolve salt in water you get a clear salty liquid. This liquid is called
a salt 'solution'.

Plan

Find out how much salt you can dissolve
in 10 cm³ water. This will be your
investigation.

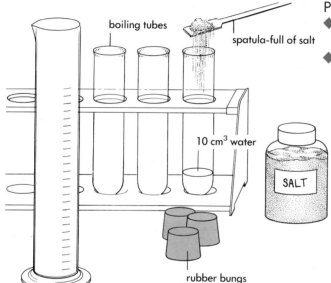

boiling tubes

spatula-full of salt

10 cm³ water

SALT

rubber bungs

clock

Add one spatula-full of salt to 10 cm³
water.
Put a stopper in the tube then shake it.
◆ How long does it take for the salt to
   dissolve?
◆ How many more spatula-fulls of salt
   will dissolve in the water? You will
   need to dissolve one spatula-full at a
   time.

When a solution is full it is called a 'saturated' solution.

▶ Make other saturated solutions using chemicals such
   as sugar, alum, and potassium chloride.

Record

▶ Make a table showing
   the chemicals you have
   investigated and how
   much of each chemical
   you needed to make
   10 cm³ of saturated
   solution.

Present

▶ Use graph or squared
   paper to make up a
   wordsquare puzzle
   from these words.

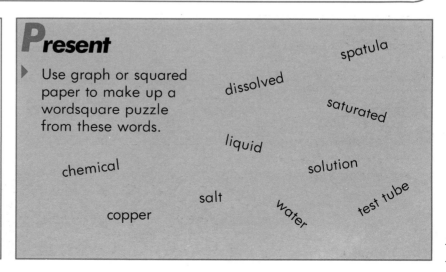

spatula

dissolved

saturated

liquid

chemical

solution

salt

water

test tube

copper

Distilling salty water

Discuss

▶ How could you tell the difference between salty water and pure water?

▶ Where would you expect to find (a) salty water (b) pure water?

Plan

You can use a chemical to tell if salt is in a water sample. The chemical is silver nitrate.

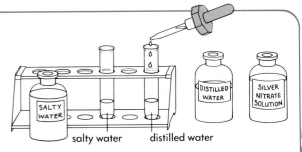

salty water   distilled water

To test for salt in water add three drops of silver nitrate solution to two water samples.

◆ What happens when you add silver nitrate solution to salty water?

◆ What happens when you add silver nitrate solution to distilled water?

Plan

Find out if you can get pure water by boiling salty water. You will be **investigating**.

Boil a sample of salt water.
Hold a plate over it and catch the drips in a small beaker.

⚠ Make sure no splashes get onto the plate.

plate held at angle

salty water

SALTY WATER

Pour the drips which you have collected into a test tube.

Test your sample to see if there is any salt in it.

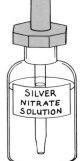

sample you collected

SILVER NITRATE SOLUTION

◆ What results do you get in this test?

Discuss

▶ How could you improve this method so that more water is collected? You are **evaluating** your investigation.

Record

▶ Copy and complete this sentence: Silver nitrate solution shows if salt is in a water sample because ....
▶ Draw and label diagrams to show how you collected the water sample.
▶ Draw and label diagrams to show how you tested your sample.

Catching the steam

Plan

You can use this apparatus to heat water, collect the steam, and then cool the steam. This method of getting a liquid sample is called 'distillation'.

Set up the apparatus so that it is steady and safe.

⚠ Boil the salt water gently.

◆ What happens?

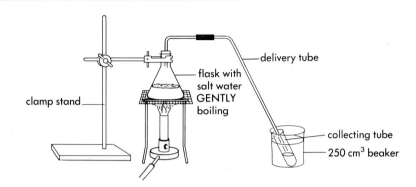

delivery tube

flask with
salt water
GENTLY
boiling

clamp stand

collecting tube

250 cm³ beaker

Lower the water bath and collecting tube away from the delivery tube *before* you stop heating the salty water.

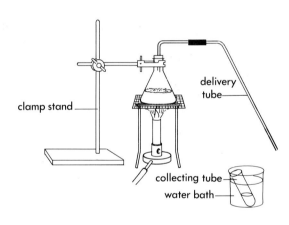

clamp stand

delivery
tube

collecting tube

water bath

◆ What does the cold water bath do to the steam in the collecting tube?

Test your sample to find out if it has salt in it.

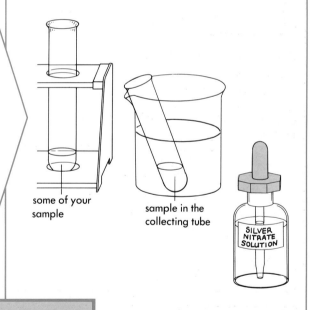

some of your
sample

sample in the
collecting tube

SILVER
NITRATE
SOLUTION

Discuss

▶ Would a hot water bath do the job as well as the cold water bath?
▶ Finula said she thought this method would work even better if the delivery tube was cooled. This was her **prediction**. Do you agree or not? Give your reasons. Make a **hypothesis** which could account for both your answers.

Record

▶ Do the exercise on Cut Out CH3.

Dyes

Some chemicals can change the colour of fabrics and fibres. These chemicals are called 'dyes'. Many plant materials contain dyes.

Discuss

▶ Think of some plant materials which would make good dyes.

Plan

⚠ You are going to make a dye bath and use it to dye some fabrics. You can use any of these plant materials to make your dye: onion skins, coloured flower petals, edible coloured berries, or turmeric powder.

1 Put some pieces of plant material in a beaker with some water.
Boil the water for about 15 minutes.

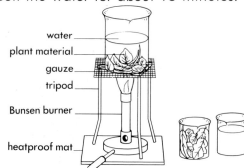

water
plant material
gauze
tripod
Bunsen burner
heatproof mat

◆ What colour changes take place?

2 Let the mixture cool.
Then filter the mixture.
You now have a dye bath.

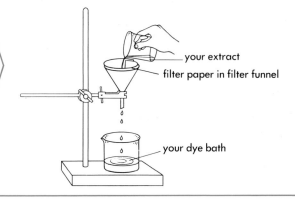

your extract
filter paper in filter funnel
your dye bath

3 Use your dye bath to dye four or five pieces of fabric.

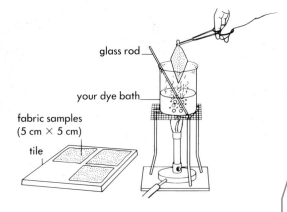

glass rod
your dye bath
fabric samples
(5 cm × 5 cm)
tile

4 Turn off the Bunsen burner.
Let the apparatus cool.
Remove your pieces of fabric and let them dry.

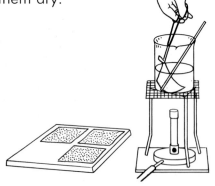

▶ Try using other dyes and different sorts of fabrics.

Present

▶ Make a display for your class notice board. Remember to show which fabrics and dyes you used.

Washing out dyes

Some dyes wash out of fabrics. 'Fast' dyes are those which do *not* wash out.

Discuss

Sofia had this idea about dyes:

> 'Hot soapy water washes out more dye than cold soapy water because temperature affects the dye'.

You can test this **hypothesis**.

▶ Here are some ideas. Read them and decide which ones you will use to test Sofia's hypothesis.

We need hot and cold soapy water.

We have to cut each fabric piece in half.

We have to give the cold soapy water longer to work.

We should use the lightest sample we have.

We have to leave the fabric in hot, soapy water for the same time as the one in cold soapy water.

We have to cut each sample into three pieces and leave one piece unwashed.

▶ Add any more ideas which you think you will need.

Plan

Use the ideas you have discussed to test Sofia's hypothesis.
Predict what you think will happen.
You can use some of the samples you have already made to carry out your **experiment**.

Record

▶ Make a list of the ideas which your group thought were important.
▶ Describe what you did and what results you got.

Plan

▶ Plan an **investigation** to find out whether detergents have the same effect as soap on plant-dyed fabrics.

Green dye from leaves

If you slip over on wet grass you may get green stains on your clothes. This is because you crush the grass when you fall on it and a green substance called 'chlorophyll' comes out. In this activity you will extract some chlorophyll and then find out more about it.

Plan

⚠ In this activity you will be using substances which can catch fire easily even if there are no flames nearby. You must use a fume cupboard to avoid any danger.

Crush all the chemicals and plant material together in the mortar with a pestle. Pour off the liquid you have made into a beaker. Store your plant extract for the next part of the task.

◆ Is there any chlorophyll in the liquid?

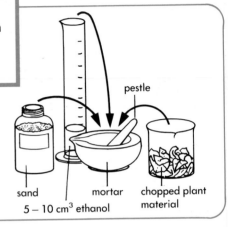

pestle

sand   mortar   chopped plant material

5 – 10 cm³ ethanol

Drop chromatography

Plan

Now you can **investigate** the chlorophyll which you have extracted using a method called 'chromatography'.

Use a thin glass tube to put one small spot of the liquid on the centre of a filter paper. Let it dry.

Do this seven or eight times more until you have a dark spot.

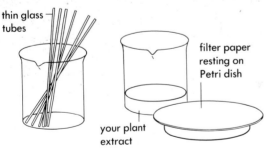

thin glass tubes

filter paper resting on Petri dish

your plant extract

◆ Has the spot spread out?

Put one drop of ethanol on the spot in the middle of the filter paper.

Watch what happens and then add more drops, one at a time. You are making a drop chromatogram.

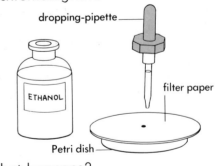

dropping-pipette

ETHANOL

filter paper

Petri dish

◆ What happens?

▶ Try using another chemical instead of ethanol. You could try acetone, water or a liquid which your teacher suggests.

Filter strip chromatography

Follow the plan

Set up a filter strip chromatogram to test your plant extract.

Draw a pencil line on your filter strip.

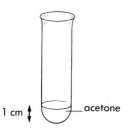

strip of filter paper

pencil line (about 2 cm from bottom)

Put one drop of your plant extract on the pencil line. Let it dry.

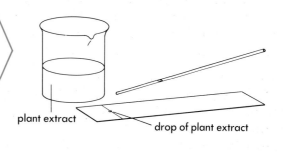

plant extract

drop of plant extract

Pour a little acetone into a test tube.

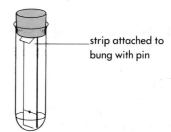

1 cm

acetone

Hang the filter strip into the test tube.

strip attached to bung with pin

Leave the filter strip until the liquid line is nearly at the top.

Discuss

▶ What have you found out about the dye from your plant extract?
▶ Is the dye from your plant extract a single substance?
▶ What other things have you found out about the dye? You are **interpreting** your results.

Present

▶ Make a poster of your group's chromatograms.
▶ On the poster, explain how you made the different chromatograms.

Plan

▶ **Investigate** the dye from other plants in a similar way and compare the chromatograms you make with your original ones.
▶ Find out more about the green colour in plants by looking at thin slices of leaves under a microscope.

Heating materials

When materials are heated changes take place. Different changes take place with different materials.

Discuss

▶ Look at your collection of materials below and discuss in your group the changes you would expect to happen if you heated each material. You may think of different things like 'it will smell'; 'it will burn with a flame'; 'it will make a noise'; 'it will melt'. These are the sorts of **predictions** you could make.

Plan

Find out how heating affects some solid materials. Practise using tongs before doing this **investigation** if you have not used them before. You might find Skill Sheet 14 useful.

Collect together a number of small samples of different materials. For example you could use cardboard, metal foil, a wooden splint, a piece of china, a piece of spaghetti, copper foil, or a nail.

⚠ Heat a small piece of each material in the Bunsen burner flame.
Watch closely what happens each time. You will be **observing**.

⚠ Put your hot tongs and your sample on a heat proof mat after you have heated each material.

Record

▶ Make a table, like the one shown here, of your predictions and observations.

Name of material	My prediction	My observation
Cardboard	It will burn with a flame.	
Tin foil		
Wooden splint		
China		

Heating materials in test tubes

Some materials are powders or crystals. You cannot easily pick them up with tongs. To find out how these materials change when they are heated you will need to use test tubes or bottle tops.

Discuss

▶ Discuss the changes you think will take place with each of the materials below, just as you did in the first investigation. You will be making more **predictions**.

Plan

Investigate how heating affects some powders and crystals.

Collect together a number of samples of different materials. You could use sugar, copper sulphate, zinc oxide, chalk, bath salts, salt, or custard powder.

Put a spatula-full of each substance in a test tube and heat this in the Bunsen burner flame.

Watch closely what happens in each case. Make careful **observations**.

⚠ Make sure that you always point the test tube away from yourself and from other people nearby when you are heating these substances.

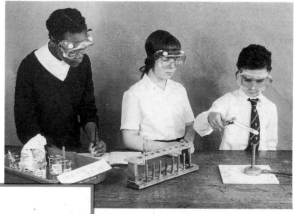

Record

▶ Add these predictions and observations to your table.

Discuss

▶ Sort out all the materials you have used in these two investigations into three groups with headings:

   materials *permanently* changed
   materials *temporarily* changed
   materials *not* changed

▶ What patterns do you see in your results?

Record

▶ Make a table with these three headings to record the way you have **classified** the materials into the three groups.

Indicators

You have probably seen indicators on cars and other vehicles. Car indicators tell you something about a car. They tell you which direction it is going in – left, right, or straight on.

There are some special chemicals which scientists also call 'indicators'. Chemical indicators can give you information about other chemicals. Litmus is a common indicator. It is made from a sort of lichen. Lichens are plants which live on the bark of trees or on concrete or stone.

Plan

Find out how litmus works as an indicator. You will be **investigating**.

Collect together a number of different chemicals.
Mix one drop of each of the chemicals with one drop of litmus *liquid*.

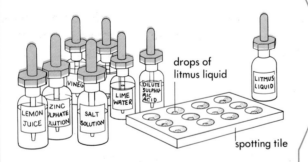

drops of litmus liquid

spotting tile

◆ What colour changes do you see? These are your **observations**.

Use litmus *paper* to test each of the chemicals.

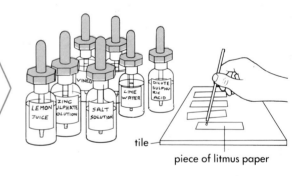

tile

piece of litmus paper

◆ Does litmus paper give the same colour changes as litmus liquid?

Record

▶ Draw a table like the one shown. Decide how many lines you need in your table.
▶ Write your results in the table.

Chemicals which turn litmus red	Chemicals which do not change the litmus colour	Chemicals which turn the litmus blue

Discuss

▶ What pattern can you see in the results?

Red cabbage extract

You may have noticed that the colour often comes out of vegetables when you boil them. Red cabbage extract is the liquid you get when you boil red cabbage in water for a few minutes. This liquid is an indicator.

Follow the plan

You are going to make some red cabbage extract and use it to test some chemicals.

Boil some red cabbage in water for a few minutes.
Let the liquid cool down before you touch the beaker.
Mix drops of this liquid with each of the chemicals which you used in your first investigation.
Make some red cabbage paper by dipping filter paper strips into the extracts and drying them.
Use one of these pieces of paper to test each of the chemicals.

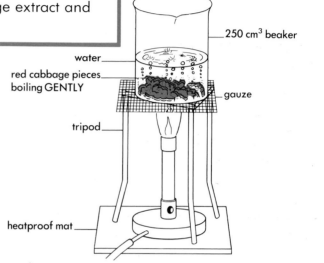

250 cm³ beaker
water
red cabbage pieces boiling GENTLY
gauze
tripod
heatproof mat

▶ Try testing an extract made from another plant. Try rose petals or fresh beetroot.

Present

▶ Draw a chart to show all your results.

Universal indicator

Universal indicator is a mixture of indicators. It is different from other indicators because it can show many more colours. Each of these colours is given a number called the 'pH value'. A pH value less than 7 means that the chemical is 'acid'.

Plan

Test each of the chemicals used in the other investigations with universal indicator paper. Watch to see what colour changes take place in each case.

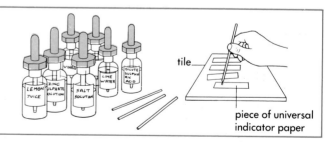

tile
piece of universal indicator paper

Record

▶ Make a table of your results, which shows the universal indicator colour and pH value for each chemical you used.

Investigating chemical changes

When you mix chemicals together you will often notice changes taking place. In this activity you will mix some liquids together and find out what different changes you notice.

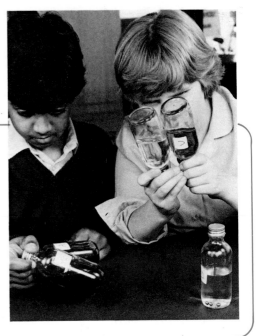

Plan

For this activity you need to make a collection of different liquid chemicals.

Label the chemicals A, B, C etc. Describe each one of them in detail.

Here are some words which you might find useful.

frothy   colourless   bitty   clear
coloured   smelly   cloudy   thick

◆ What other **observations** could you make?

Bits in liquids

You will probably have noticed that some liquids look cloudy when they are mixed. They have bits of solid chemical mixed in with the liquid. It is possible to separate the solid bits from the liquid so that you have a clear liquid with all the bits at the bottom. These bits are called a 'precipitate'.

cloudy liquid

some time later →

clear liquid

precipitate

Plan

Find out what changes take place when you mix different chemicals together. You will be **investigating**.

Pour samples of two chemicals A and B into two separate test tubes. Each tube should be about ¼ full.

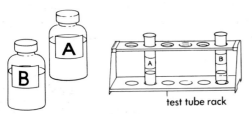

test tube rack

Mix the two chemicals together.

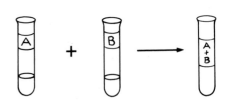

◆ Does a precipitate form?
Observe the results carefully.

Record

▶ Make a table which describes what the chemicals looked like before, during, and after you mixed them.
Your table will show your **observations**.

▶ Try mixing A with three more chemicals, C, D, and E, in the same way. Try all the combinations – AC, AD, AE.
Try other combinations

Metal reactions

Plan

Find out what changes take place when you mix iron filings or powder with liquid copper sulphate. You will be **investigating**.

Add a spatula-full of iron filings to some copper sulphate solution. Stir the mixture slowly.

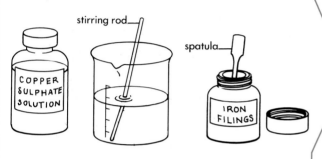

- ◆ What colour changes do your see?
- ◆ What happens as you add more filings?

Filter your mixture.

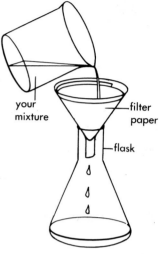

your mixture — filter paper — flask

- ◆ What is left on the filter paper?
- ◆ What colour is the liquid left in the flask? Keep this liquid for your next investigation.

Record

▶ Draw a diagram and colour it to show what you started with and what you ended up with.

Discuss

▶ Use the information given below to check what substances you started with.
▶ What substances do you think were formed at the end of your investigation? You are **interpreting** the information.
▶ What do you think has happened during this investigation? This will be your **inference**.

Information
Copper sulphate solution is a blue liquid.
Iron filings are dark grey specks.
Iron sulphate solution is a green liquid.
Copper powder is dark reddish-brown in colour.

Plan

Investigate what happens when you react magnesium ribbon with copper sulphate solution or iron sulphate solution.

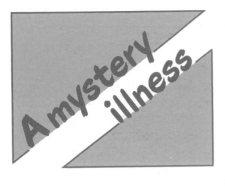

A mystery illness

Minimata is a town on a bay on the coast of Japan. Fishing is its oldest industry but now there are also many factories. In 1952 a mystery illness struck the people and their animals.

Towards the end of 1952, and during the beginning of 1953, the people of Minimata found that some pets fell ill. In December 1953 one person died of the illness. Then many more people died and more became disabled. Many other animals – fish and sea-birds – were affected. People could not work out the cause of the illness.

Record

▶ Use the chart to work out how many people died from the illness each year.
▶ Record the numbers in a table like the one shown here. Work out how many more lines you need.

year	Number of people who died in Minimata of the mystery illness
1949	0
1950	0

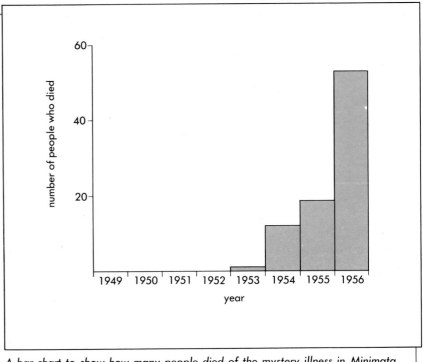

A bar chart to show how many people died of the mystery illness in Minimata

Finding the cause

The people of Minimata asked local scientists to help find the cause of the illness. The scientists started work in 1956. They listened to the things that local people had noticed over the years. Here are the **observations** they made.

Observations

The water in the bay had slowly become more and more dirty during the last three or four years.

Fishing families first found the symptoms in their pets in 1952, about the same time as people had started to find dead fish in the bay.

More people were dying from the illness each year.

Factories put waste into the water in the bay and also one factory started making large amounts of a plastic (PVC) in 1952.

Discuss

▶ How many different observations had the people made?

The 'poisoned fish' idea

The scientists worked on several ideas. One of them was the 'poisoned fish' idea. This was their **hypothesis**. They thought that fish in the bay were being poisoned by a chemical being put into the bay by the PVC factory.

Trying to stop the illness

In 1956, scientists said that no-one should fish from the bay anymore.

Record

▶ Do the exercise on Cut Out CH4.
▶ List some suggestions you could make to stop any more people getting the mystery illness.
▶ Write a letter to the people of Minimata giving your ideas.

Record

Look at the chart showing how many people died before and after 1956.
▶ Record in a table the number of people who died from the illness each year.
▶ Decide whether or not the fishing ban of 1956 worked.
You are **interpreting** the information.

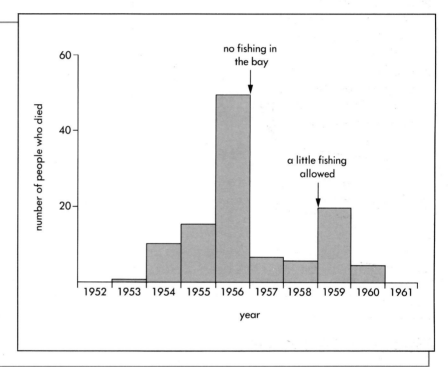

Present

▶ Use Cut Out CH5 to make up a collage to show what life might have been like in Minimata.

Poisonous chemicals

The scientists worked out that poisonous chemicals used to make PVC were getting into the water from the factory. These chemicals contained mercury and this caused the mystery illness. The factory is no longer allowed to release these chemicals into the bay.

Record

▶ Find out about another chemical disaster. Look in books and newspapers.
▶ Write a short story about it.

Pesticides

Here are two different meanings for the word 'pest'.
A pest is a child who is being naughty.
A pest is an animal which harms you or your environment or any of the plants and animals you need.

Discuss

The pictures show some examples that fit the second meaning of the word pest.
▶ Try to think of some more.

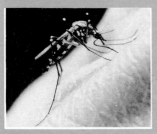
Mosquitoes which carry the disease malaria are pests.

Rats which eat the grain we store are pests.

Slugs which eat the green vegetables we grow are pests.

Cockroaches in kitchens are pests.

Killing pests with chemicals

Chemicals which kill pests are called 'pesticides'. Since 1940 many new chemicals have been made to kill pests efficiently. When these chemicals were first used people did not think about the effects they might have. Now they know that pesticides can harm other living creatures too. DDT is a pesticide that was once used a lot. It has been used to kill many types of pests – food pests, forest pests, and mosquitoes.

DDT is spread using hand sprays, large machine sprays or aeroplanes for very large areas.

Discuss

▶ Use the information you have read to decide whether each of these statements *is true*, *may be true*, or *is false*. You will be **classifying**.

Cockroaches are pests.
DDT is a chemical which kills pests.
DDT gets washed down into the soil when it rains.

Pests are living things.
Grain we store for food is a pest.
Pests are chemicals we spray on the land.

Pesticides are useful to us because they kill pests.
Pesticides might kill other things apart from pests.

Record

▶ Write out each sentence and record your decision beside it.

Solving one problem ...

DDT was used to kill many kinds of crop pests all over the world.

... creating another

However in areas where DDT had been used people noticed that animals, birds, and fish were dying. These were their **observations**. Scientists **investigated** water samples and some of the dead animals to try to find out what was wrong. They found DDT in the water and in the bodies of the animals. They then worked out a set of **hypotheses**.

1 DDT which is sprayed on the land drains through the soil into nearby streams and rivers.
2 When small fish eat the water plants they eat DDT too.
3 Larger fish eat the small fish so they eat DDT too.
4 Birds that eat a lot of fish have a very large amount of DDT in their bodies. Their eggs are damaged by the DDT in their bodies.
5 DDT stays in animals' bodies for a very long time.

Record

▶ Do the exercise on Cut Out CH6.

Present

▶ Plan and present a debate about whether or not pesticides should be sprayed in an area. Some examples of the sort of people who might be involved are given below. You could add others, for example a farm adviser, a bird watcher, or someone who has an allotment.

For years my crops have been damaged by pests. Since I have sprayed them there is much less damage. I can't afford to stop spraying: people want their food to be as cheap as possible.

The old type of sprays had lots of bad effects. What we need is good pesticides which only kill the pests and do no other harm. The problem is that we can't always tell exactly what happens when we start spraying a new chemical.

We should not kill any animals or plants. They should all be allowed to live. We should let the natural balance of plants and animals live together.

My friends and I have fished here for years. We enjoy being out in the country. In the last few years the number of fish in the river has become much less. We also see far fewer birds near the river bank.

Pests take food from people so even if we do have problems with one pesticide a new one will soon be invented. We must keep trying to find better and better ones all the time.

Record

An atlas will help you to do these tasks.
▶ Look carefully at this map. Cut out the map from Cut Out CH7 and fix it in your work book.
▶ Label the main oceans and seas.
▶ Pencil in the names of the countries you know.
▶ Use the atlas to label more countries.
▶ Make a list of places which have no salt mines and which are a long way from sea water.

Discuss

▶ Read the passages opposite.
▶ Discuss what words fit in the spaces.

Record

▶ Write out the passages in your work book and fill in the spaces with the words you have thought of.

Did you know?

Salt is vital to your health. You must have a certain amount of salt in your body (not too much, not too little) so that your nerves and muscles work properly.

Salt is an important chemical because it can be used to make other chemicals like glass and soap.

Salt is used to melt ice on roads.

People obtain salt in a variety of ways depending on where they live and what is found there. In the UK, and in some other countries, salt is dug up from salt mines. Salt can also be obtained from sea water, swamp water, spring water and plants.

Salt crystals

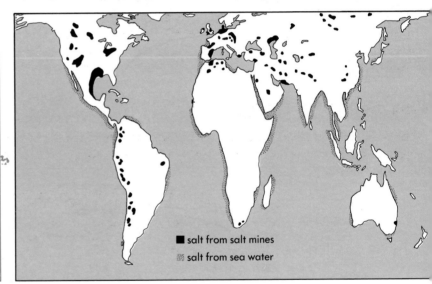

■ salt from salt mines
▦ salt from sea water

Salt around the world

Ways of obtaining salt from sea water

Sea water is pumped into huge shallow lakes near the shore. The Sun then slowly dries up the water and _____ the salt behind. The salt then has to be _____ up and transported to where it will be used. _____ may be used to make other chemicals in a _____ or it may be used in people's homes. It _____ also be sent to a market to be sold.

Salt from mines

The map shows part of the world where there are rocks containing salt. This is called 'rock salt'. It is _____ ou of the ground and then it _____ to be purified. This means separating the _____ from the other bits of rock and _____

Salt from plants

All plants contain some salt. In places a long way from the sea or salt mines people get salt for cooking from plants. Leonard and Mwila from Zambia did a project on how people can do this.

They burnt some plant leaves and collected the ashes. These ashes had salt in them but there were also other substances which they did not want. They had to separate the salt from these other substances. They used a separating method to get the salt on its own. The diagram shows what they did.

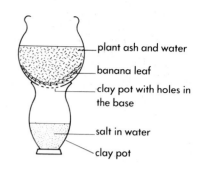

plant ash and water

banana leaf

clay pot with holes in the base

salt in water

clay pot

Discuss

▶ Suggest how people use the clay pots and banana leaves to get salt from the ashes. You are **inferring**.
▶ How do you think they get the salt crystals from the liquid in the bottom of the clay pot? This will be your **prediction**.

Record

▶ Draw your own diagram of the apparatus that Leonard and Mwila used.
▶ Do the exercise on Cut Out CH8 (part 1).

The salty spring

Luke lives in Finduwa in Papua New Guinea. He did a project about the way people in his village used to get salt from nearby salty streams.

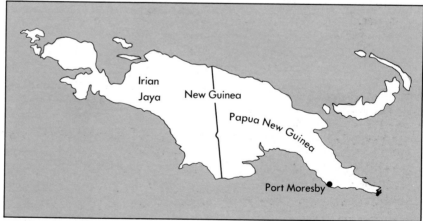

Papua New Guinea, where Luke lives

Discuss

▶ Read his account of the project in Cut Out CH8 (part 2).
▶ Discuss what you think Luke means when he uses the following words in his account:
'a spring'
'a thick bush'
'dry season'
'wet season'
'lets a bit of water dry'.

Record

▶ Cut out Luke's account from Cut Out CH8 and fix it neatly in your work book.
▶ Underline in pencil all the things that the villagers had to do to get the salt. The first one has been done for you.

3.12

Separating chemicals

Separating sand and salt from water

Many substances are found mixed with water. There are various ways in which the substances can be separated from the water. You can **investigate** the best way to do this for sand and water and salt and water.

Record

▶ Look carefully at the three separating methods shown in the plan box below.
▶ Write down what you think will happen to the water in each case.
▶ Write down what you think will happen to the sand and to the salt in each method.

These will be your **predictions**.

Plan

Try out the three separation methods below. You will need three sand/water mixtures and three salt/water mixtures.

This activity may take longer than one lesson so plan your work carefully. Talk to your teacher about this.

Filter method

Pouring off method

collecting beaker

sand/water or salt/water mixture

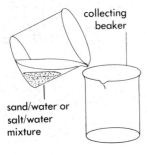

filter paper

funnel

sand/water or salt/water mixture

conical flask

Evaporation method

tongs

top of Petri dish

sand/water or salt/water mixture

◆ Did you lose any of the sand or salt?

◆ Did you lose any of the sand or salt?

◆ Did you lose any of the sand or salt?

Discuss

▶ Were your predictions correct?
▶ Which method is the quickest for each mixture?
▶ Which method is the simplest for each mixture?
▶ Which method is best if you want to collect the sand?
▶ Which method is best if you want to collect: just the sand; just the salt; or just the water?
You are **evaluating** each method.

Record

▶ Draw a table showing what happened to the sand, the salt and the water in each method.

A mixture of sand salt and water

Suppose you had a mixture of sand *and* salt in water. Caroline's group were given such a mixture. They discussed whether the three methods of separation would work. They made this **prediction**:

'The filter method will not work by itself.'

Discuss

▶ Do you agree or disagree with Caroline's group's prediction?
▶ **Predict** what will happen using the three separating methods for the sand, salt and water mixture.

Plan

Test your predictions.
You will be **experimenting**.

Discuss

▶ Were your predictions correct?
▶ Which method do you think must be used to separate sand and salt from water, if they are mixed together, if you want to collect *both* the sand and the salt.

    These will be your **evaluations**.

Record

▶ Draw some labelled diagrams to explain how you would separate sand and salt from a mixture of salt, sand and water.
▶ Draw up a table to say what happens to the sand, the salt and the water in each case.

Stomach acid

Your stomach juice contains many things including hydrochloric acid. Sometimes you may feel unwell because there is too much acid in your stomach juice. You could use stomach powder or stomach tablets to take away the extra acid. One chemical in stomach powders or stomach tablets is sodium bicarbonate.

Plan

What happens when you take stomach tablets? Find out by looking at what happens when sodium bicarbonate is added to hydrochloric acid.
In all these **investigations** you will be using bromophenol blue indicator.

Measure out 50 cm³ hydrochloric acid in a small flask.
Add a pipette-full of indicator.

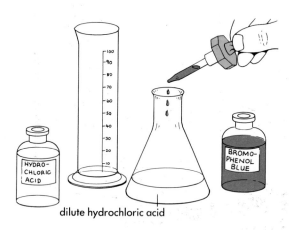

dilute hydrochloric acid

◆ What colour changes do you notice?

Add a spatula-full of sodium bicarbonate to the acid and gently shake the flask.

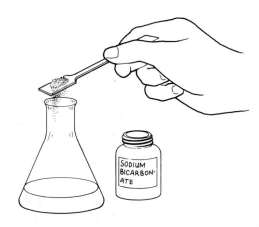

◆ How many spatulas-full of sodium bicarbonate do you need to change the colour?

Record

▶ Make a table like this of your **observations**:

Sodium bicarbonate spatulas-full	Colour	Other observations
O		
1		

▶ Record the colour of bromophenol blue indicator in acid and in a solution with no acid.
▶ Record everything else that happened in the flask during the investigation.

Discuss

▶ What **inferences** can you make from your results?
▶ What do you think you have found out?

Investigating stomach tablets

Stomach tablets and mixtures contain sodium bicarbonate, or other chemicals which work in the same way. This **investigation** will help you find out more about stomach tablets.

Plan

In this investigation you must weigh the chemicals accurately. You are going to compare a type of stomach tablet with pure sodium bicarbonate.

Weigh an Alka-Seltzer tablet, and then break it into small pieces in a Petri dish.
Measure 50 cm^3 hydrochloric acid into a 100 cm^3 beaker.
Put a pipette-full of indicator into the beaker.
Add bits of the tablet and stir.
Stop adding bits when the colour changes.
Weigh the bits of tablet left.

Find out how much sodium bicarbonate you need to use up the same amount of acid.

Record

▶ Record all your results. You can find the amount of tablet used up by the acid by subtraction:

Weight of whole tablet	− Weight left	= Weight used
4.3g	− 1.6g	= 2.7g

Discuss

▶ Which was better at using up the acid, the stomach tablet or sodium bicarbonate? Why do you think so?
▶ How fair is it to just use this chemical test to measure how good the tablet is? You are **evaluating**.

Present

▶ Make an advertisement for a stomach tablet using the things you have found out.

Using chemicals safely

Working with chemicals can be dangerous if you do not take care. You should always make sure that you take all the correct safety measures when you work with chemicals.

Discuss

Here are some photographs of people using chemicals in the laboratory.
► Look carefully at each one.
► Which photographs show people working safely?
► What are the pupils doing which is unsafe in the other photographs?

Record

► Record what you think the pupils are doing in each photograph.
If they are not working safely, record what they are doing wrong and how they should change the way they work to make it safe.

Present

► Use your ideas to design a poster to put on the wall with the title 'Using Chemicals Safely'.

Hazard warning labels

Hazard labels tell you to be careful, something may be dangerous. Here are some examples of hazard warning labels used on chemicals. You might have seen them before.

BIOHAZARD

CORROSIVE

EXPLOSIVE

FLAMMABLE

HARMFUL

POISON

Record

▶ Do the exercise on Cut Out CH9.

Hazardous chemicals

Imagine that you are working in a laboratory and you discover two new chemicals. They both cause certain things to happen and you will have to give a warning of this. The first chemical affects your voice and speech so you sound like a parrot! The second chemical makes you shrink and it can take you about a week to recover!

Present

Design hazard warning labels for each of these imaginary chemicals.
Put your designs on a large poster with those of the rest of your class.
Ask your teacher for samples of household and laboratory containers. Make a chart which shows the name of the product and any hazard warnings on the container.

Record

This cartoon comes from a book called 'Safety in Laboratories'.

▶ Draw a similar cartoon (or trace over this one) in your work book.
▶ Write a caption for the drawing.
▶ Find some other examples of hazard warning labels and list and draw them in your work book.
▶ Look out for examples of places where you see hazard warning labels in use. Write them down and say where you saw them.

3.15

Chemicals — some useful words

ABS	compound	iodine	polythene
acid	concentration	iron	pure
acidic	copper	irritant	PVC
acrylic	cordial	insecticide	quinine
air	corrosive	melt	reaction
alchemy	dangerous	medicine	rocket
alcohol	DDT	laxative	rodenticide
alkali	detergent	liquid	safe
alkaline	diesel	magnesium	silk
alloy	dissolve	malleable	smelling salts
aluminium	drug	mercury	slippery
anaesthetic	ductile	mixture	soap
anhydrous	effervescence	nails	solid
antibiotic	exhaust fumes	natural	solution
antiseptic	explosive	neutral	solvent
asbestos	fermentation	nicotine	steel
aspirin	fertilizers	nitrogen	sticky
bacteriocide	firework	nylon	sugar
Bakelite	foods	oil	sulphur
blood	freeze	oxygen	suspension
boil	fuel	paint	tea
brittle	gas	paper	tin
caustic	glucose	paracetamol	TNT
chemist	hair	pesticide	tranquilizer
chromatography	helium	petrol	washing-up liquid
chromium	herbicide	pharmacist	water
coffee	herbalist	plasma	wool
coloured	hydrogen	plastics	zinc
colourless	indicator	poison	
cotton	ink	pollution	

Communication

Contents

Body language	4.1
Building your own radio	4.2
Hearing	4.3
Illusions	4.4
Messages	4.5
Noise	4.6
Sight	4.7
Special signals	4.8
The speed of sound	4.9
Talking	4.10
Telephones	4.11
Ultrasound	4.12
Whale talk	4.13
Why birds sing	4.14
Your ear	4.15
Communication – some useful words	4.16

Symbols you will find:

These are things you should try to do.

These are extra things to do if you have time.

These are questions to think about when you are planning practical work.

When you see this symbol you need to take extra care.

This theme contains 15 spreads which can be worked through in any order.

Theme 4

Body language

Everybody communicates without talking by using 'body language'. You use body language by the way you dress, the gestures you make, the expression on your face, the way you stand and your hairstyle. All these things signal messages about yourself. The meanings different people get from these signals may not always be the same.

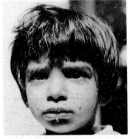

Discuss

▶ Discuss each picture.
▶ Decide what each person is communicating about themselves. You are making **interpretations**.
▶ What body language are they using to do this?
▶ What messages are they sending using body language?
▶ Decide if everyone in your group receives the same messages about these pictures.
▶ Do any of the pictures make you have any strong feelings?

Gestures

You often use gestures to communicate with other people.

Discuss

▶ Discuss the different ways people greet one another throughout the world.
▶ Carefully watch each person in another group without them noticing. Discuss what body language they are using to communicate with each other.
▶ What do the gestures tell you about how the person is feeling?

Present

▶ In your group use gestures to communicate these ideas to each other:
'stay here'   'yes'
'go over there'
'don't do that'
'go away quickly'
'goodbye'   'no'
'I'm fed up with you'
'I agree'
▶ Try some other ideas.

Facial expressions

The expression on your face can also communicate to other people how you feel about things.

Discuss

▶ What do you notice about the eyes, eyebrows, mouth, and skin in each face below? These are your **observations**.
▶ Discuss what feelings these faces are communicating. These are your **interpretations**.

 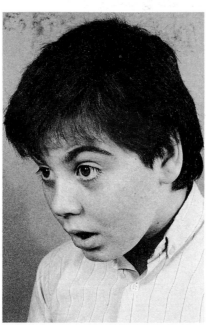 

Present

▶ Express the following feelings or emotions to your group using different expressions: worry; impatience; contentment; anger; sadness.
▶ Try some others.
▶ Use Cut Out CM1 to make faces with different expressions.
▶ In pairs, choose one of the following situations and act it out to the rest of your group. Use the sorts of body language that describe each situation best.

> Two young children are very frightened of something and are hiding.

> Two friends are walking around feeling very bored.

> A woman's pet dog has just died. Her husband is comforting her.

> A couple have just heard they have won the 'pools'.

Discuss

▶ What body language did you use for each situation?
▶ How did the body language you use help to make the situation more real?

Building your own radio

Discuss

▶ What kinds of message do you receive by listening to the radio?
▶ What sort of message could you send using a radio transmitter?

Follow the plan

You are going to build a very simple radio. It is so simple it does not even need a battery.

You will need to be able to solder to build this radio. If you have not done any soldering before, use Skill Sheet 11 to help you.

Follow each step carefully.

When you have finished your radio it should look like the one in the photo.

1	2	3
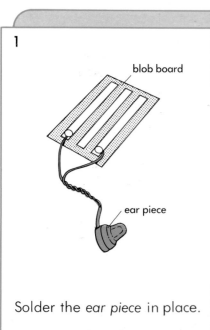		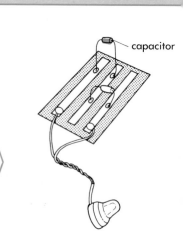
Solder the *ear piece* in place.	Solder the *diode* in place.	Solder the *capacitor* in place.

blob board

ear piece

diode

capacitor

4

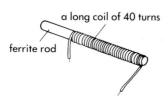

a long coil of 40 turns

ferrite rod

Wind 40 turns of insulated wire around one
end of the ferrite rod.

a short coil of 5 turns

Wind five turns of insulated wire around the
other end of the ferrite rod.

5 Strip the ends of the wires using the wire
strippers.

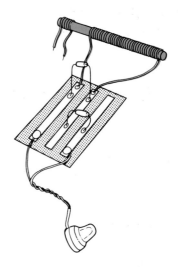

Solder the long coil in place.

6

aerial

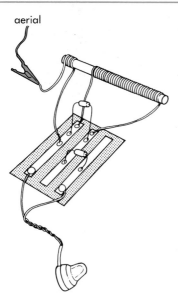

Solder one end of the short coil in place.

Connect the other end to the aerial.

7

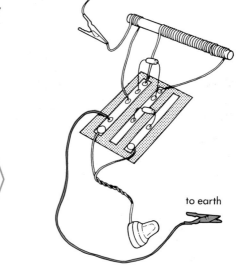

to earth

Solder the earth wire in place.

Connect the other end to an 'earth'.
If your radio does not work, ask your
teacher for help.

Plan

Investigate what happens when you move the ferrite rod *slowly* in and out of the long
coil. Keep the small coil in place while you move the ferrite rod. You will need to listen
with the ear piece.

Hearing

Some people can hear sounds more easily than others.

Plan

Find out how well each person in your group can hear. You can design your own test or use the ideas below to help you plan your **investigation**.

Move away until the blindfolded person can no longer hear the sound.

Now move back towards the blindfolded person. Check when they can hear the sound again.

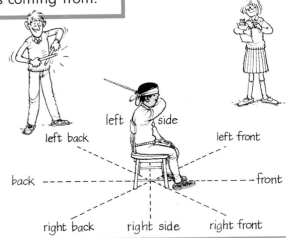

◆ Why was the person blindfolded?
◆ Does it make a difference if one ear is covered? (Use ear muffs to investigate this.)
◆ Do different noises produce different results?

Plan

Find out if a person can tell where a noise is coming from.

Bang two sticks together and ask a blindfolded person to point to where they think the noise is coming from. Move around and make the noise in all of the eight positions shown in the diagram.

◆ Is this a fair test?
◆ Does it make a difference if one ear is covered?
◆ Does distance make a difference?
◆ Do different noises give different results?
You are **interpreting** your **observations**.

left side
left back   left front
back ------ ------front
right back   right side   right front

Discuss

▶ Were your investigations fair tests?
▶ What criticisms can you make of these investigations?
▶ Use your **evaluations** to decide how you can improve your investigations.

Record

▶ Record the results from your investigations.
▶ Describe briefly what you did.
▶ Make a list of your criticisms.

Improving your hearing

Plan

Here are three devices which are easy to make. Do an **investigation** to find out how each one could help to improve your hearing.

Ear trumpet

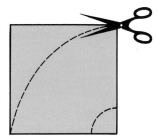

cone

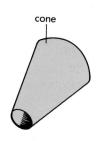

Cut a piece of paper as shown above.

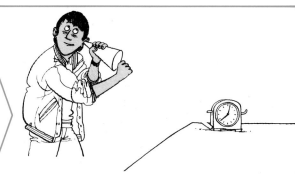

Roll the paper into a cone and fix it with sellotape.

Listening tube

Make a long tube. You could try using a listening tube in each ear.

Stethoscope

⚠ Join a large plastic funnel to some plastic tubing. Disinfect the plastic tubes before putting them in your ears.

Discuss

► When do you think these devices would be used? You are making some **inferences**.
► What other devices have you seen which are used to improve hearing?
► Did all three of the devices above improve your hearing?
► Did you need to change any of the designs?
► Which one worked best with quiet sounds?

Record

► Make a record of your investigation and of what you found out.

4.3

Illusions

Your sense of sight is very important to you, but sometimes it can be misleading. In this spread you will find that things are not always what they seem!

Finding your blind spot

Follow the plan

In each eye you have a 'blind spot'. This is a small part of your eye which cannot see. In this **investigation** you should become aware of your blind spot.

Close your left eye. Look hard at the cross. Hold the page at arms' length, with the cross in front of your open eye. Move the page very slowly towards you.

Now try it with your right eye closed.

◆ What happens?
◆ Can you compare each other's results? Try making some measurements to help you.
◆ Is the effect the same for both eyes?
◆ How could you find the blind spot in your left eye?

Discuss

Read this statement.

'At first the short line disappears. Then, as you bring the page nearer your eye, the short line comes back but the gap disappears and you see one long line.

▶ How many people in your group agree with this statement?
▶ At what stage of the investigation do they agree with it?
▶ Why do you think this happens? You are making an **inference**.

Using eyes and hands together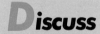

Drinking from a glass or eating a meal may seem easy. But to do these things your hands and eyes must work together. When you were a small child it took you a long time to learn these skills but now you can do them without thinking. You are going to do some 'mirror drawings'. Doing these drawings will show you how you learn to coordinate your eyes and hands.

Follow the plan

Time how long it takes you to draw between the two outlines of the first star shape on Cut Out CM2.

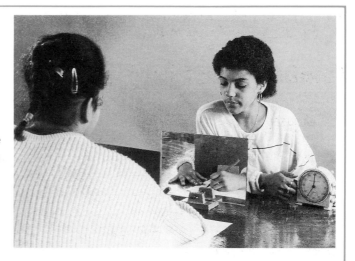

Now set up a mirror so that you can see the reflection of a second star shape. Use a piece of card to prevent you seeing the star on the page.
Time how long it takes you to draw between the two outlines of this star.
Watch what you are doing in the mirror.
Try again with fresh stars

Record

▶ Record how long it took to trace around each star.
▶ Record how often you crossed the outline of each star.
▶ Answer these questions.
   What changes did you notice after you had drawn more stars? Did your drawings become more accurate? Did you become faster?

Judging by appearances

Follow the plan

Collect the tray of containers but do NOT touch them yet.
Look carefully at the containers.
List the containers in order of weight, starting with the one you think is heaviest.
You are making **inferences** about the containers.
Now pick up the containers and estimate their weight again.
Use this information to make a second list.

◆ How can you test if your order is correct?

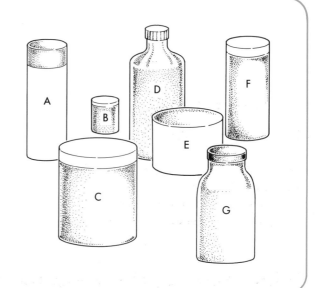

Record

▶ Record which results surprised you and give your reasons.

Messages

Everyday you send and receive messages from all sorts of different people. The messages are sent in many different ways. The way you choose to send a message depends upon a lot of things. Here are some questions you might think about.

How far does the message have to travel?
How quickly does it need to arrive?
How long is the message?
What methods are available for sending the message?
Will it need a reply?

Discuss

Discuss all the messages which people in your group have received in the last three days.
For each message decide:
▶ how it was sent
▶ how far it travelled to get to you
▶ how long it was
▶ whether or not it needed a reply
▶ how much you think it cost to send.
You may have to make **inferences** to answer some of these questions.

Sending messages

Throughout history, people have used many different ways to send messages. Some of them are shown here in the drawings.

Record

▶ Read Cut Out CM3. Make a list of all the methods you could use to send each of the messages described. Look at the drawings above for some ideas.

▶ Write down how long you think the messages would take to arrive using each of the methods on your list.

▶ Make a list of the equipment you would need in each case.

▶ Write down how much you think each method would cost in each case. You are **applying** what you know.

Discuss

▶ Think of the methods you could have used 100 years ago to send the messages described in Cut Out CM3.

▶ Decide in your group which method you think you would use nowadays to send each of the messages.

Present

▶ Read number 4 on Cut Out CM3. Design the message and how you would send it from the island described. Present this to the class.

▶ Do the same for one of the other messages.

Noise

The world is full of noise, made up of many different sounds. This noise affects how you live and work every day.

Noise and memory

Discuss

▶ Do you work best in a quiet room, or do you like to have some background noise?
▶ What sort of noises do you think people like to work with?

A group of pupils wanted to see if it was more difficult to memorize long numbers in a noisy room than in a quiet room. This is how they did their **investigation**.

Each person went somewhere quiet and was given two 7-digit numbers to memorize. They were allowed to study the numbers for ten seconds. Two minutes later they were asked to write down the numbers from memory. Next they were given two different numbers but this time they tried to learn the numbers in a noisy room. Again they were asked to write down the numbers after two minutes.

Plan

Try this investigation in your group.

◆ Does it make a difference if you work with the noisy background before the quiet background?
◆ Do different types of noise make a difference to the results? Try using different things to make a noise. Try using head-phones and a tape recorder to play different types of music in the background.
◆ Does it matter what you are trying to memorize? Try using word lists or short poems instead of the numbers. You will be **interpreting** your results.

6709418   4197420
329473   1982053
418308| 5075182
2543847   2163294
6218059   0473812
    7929131

Here are some 7-digit numbers to start you off. You can make up more of your own.

Record

▶ Record your results in a table.

Discuss

▶ Compare your results with your first discussion. Should you change the way in which you work?

Present

▶ Draw charts and diagrams to show all that you have found out from your investigation. Display these together on a large sheet of paper.

eaf animals?

'I wonder if noise affects earthworms,' said Fiona.
'Why's that?' asked Rashid.
'Well,' replied Fiona 'there are lots of worms in my garden where it's quiet but none in the road where it's noisy.' This was Fiona's **observation**.
'There are lots of other things that might affect worms being in the garden but not in the road. I don't even know if worms can hear,' said Rashid.

Discuss

▶ Rashid thought there might be other things to account for Fiona's observation that there are few worms in the road. What 'other things' could you suggest? You will be making **hypotheses**.
▶ How would you **investigate** Rashid's **question** 'Can worms hear'?

Plan

Try doing the investigation.

⚠ Remember that you will be working with living things during this investigation. You should always handle them with care and respect.

Discuss

▸ Does sound affect other small animals, such as snails and woodlice?
▸ Some people believe that sound affects the way plants grow. This is a **hypothesis**. What sort of **experiment** could you do to test this hypothesis?

Record

▶ List the things that your group thinks might affect where earthworms are found.
▶ Write a description of your investigation into the question 'Can worms hear?'.
▶ Record the answer you now have to this question. You will be **interpreting** the results of the investigation.

Sight

One of the most important ways you receive messages is by seeing. In the following activities you will find out how you see.

Record

▶ Record your first discussion using a tape recorder or by making notes.

Discuss

▶ Think of a situation when you could not see anything at all.
▶ Why do you think you could not see anything in this situation?
▶ In this diagram the girl is reading a book. If the light was turned off she would not be able to read. Why do you think this is so?
▶ What do you think is happening between the book, the bulb, and the girl's eyes? You have now made some **inferences**.
▶ Did you all agree in your group or did you have different ideas?
▶ If you had different ideas, which were the most common?

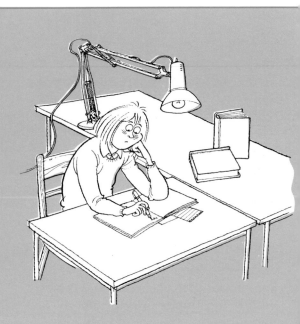

Record

▶ Make some diagrams to explain what you think is happening between the book, the bulb, and the girl's eyes.

Plan

Test your ideas about how you think you see a book. You may find it easier to work in a dark room. You will be **experimenting**.

◆ Does it make a difference where the light is in the room?
◆ Does it make a difference where you are in the room?
◆ Does it make a difference where the book is in the room?

You are making **observations** and **interpreting** them.

Discuss

► Listen to the tape or look at the notes of your first discussion again.

► Do you still agree with your ideas about what was happening between the bulb, the book, and the girl's eyes? You might want to change some of your inferences.

► These diagrams show what some pupils thought was happening. With which ones do you agree?

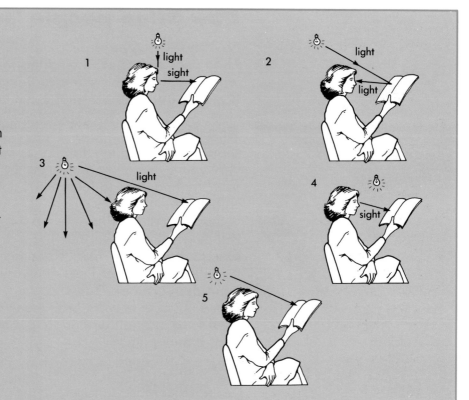

► These statements were made by students to explain how the girl could read. Compare them with your own inferences. With which ones do you agree?

The light goes from the bulb to the book so she can see it.

Her eyes send out rays and when they hit the book they come back and she can see it.

She can see the book because the light makes the book bright.

The sight from her eyes goes to the book so she can see it.

...e can see the book because the light is ...rned on.

Light moves and hits the book. It is reflected into her eyes so she can read.

The light hits her eyes and reflects her sight to the book.

When the light is on, her eyes get the reflected light back from the book.

Plan

► You may want to try out some more ideas.

Record

► Draw the picture which best describes what you think happens.
► Record the statement which best describes what you think happens.
► Describe what you think happens when people see. You are making your own **hypothesis**.

How blind people 'see'

For hundreds of years people have tried to find ways for blind people to read. The earliest record is 600 years ago when a blind Arabic professor invented a way to identify his books by using his sense of touch.

Braille

Louis Braille, who lived in Paris, went blind when he was very young. When he was older he invented a system which uses the fingertips to feel raised dots on paper. This is now called 'braille'.

Some people find braille too difficult to learn, particularly if they go blind when they are old. These people may be able to read 'moon'. This is another system for blind people to use. It is made up of lines and curves, not dots. It is easier to learn than braille.

It is possible to write braille as well as read it. Braille is used for almost all written languages, including music, maths, and science.

Discuss

▶ In your group discuss how you could make life easier for blind people in your school.

Present

▶ Imagine you are blind. Write a story about doing an everyday activity, like eating your lunch or making a cup of tea, without using your eyes.

The braille alphabet

The braille alphabet is based on six dots, like the design on a domino. The position of each dot is important. (The lines are only given in the picture to make it clear where each dot is.)

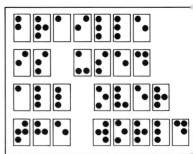

Record

▶ Use the alphabet to work out the sentence on the right, which is written in braille.
▶ Write your name, and the names of the other people in your group, in braille.
▶ Write some other words in braille and ask the rest of your group to work them out.
▶ Do the exercise on Cut Out CM4.

How deaf people 'hear'

Deaf people can communicate using finger-spelling and sign language. They can also learn to lip-read and speak.

Finger-spelling

In finger-spelling, each word is spelt out using different positions of the fingers and hands for each letter of the alphabet.

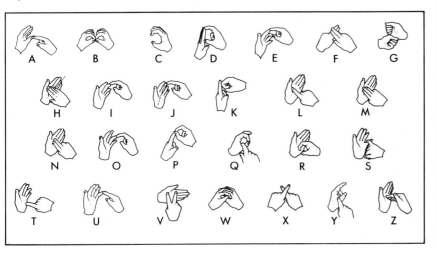

Present

▶ Use the finger-spelling alphabet to 'spell' some words to the rest of your group. See how many of these each of you can work out: eye; ear; nose; mouth; teeth; bones; hair; nail; skin; finger; heart; eyelash.
▶ Think of some more words and ask the rest of the group to **interpret** them.

Sign language

In sign language, different signs are used for different words and phrases.

Record

▶ Match each sign with one of the words below:
   good; small; friend; love; radio; books; sleep; me.
   As you do this, you will be **interpreting** the photographs.

The speed of sound

Wendy was bouncing a ball across the playground during lesson time, so the playground was very quiet. She noticed an echo. 'The ball makes a sound when it hits the ground. The echo is this sound being reflected back from the school wall', Wendy thought. This was her **inference**. 'If I could time how long it takes for me to hear the echo, I could work out how quickly sound moves'. Wendy discussed this idea with her science group and they decided to try it.

What they did

This is how they did their **investigation**. They found a high brick wall in front of which was a large, open space. There were no other buildings nearby. They stood 60 metres in front of the wall. They banged blocks of wood together to make a loud noise. They listened for the echo.

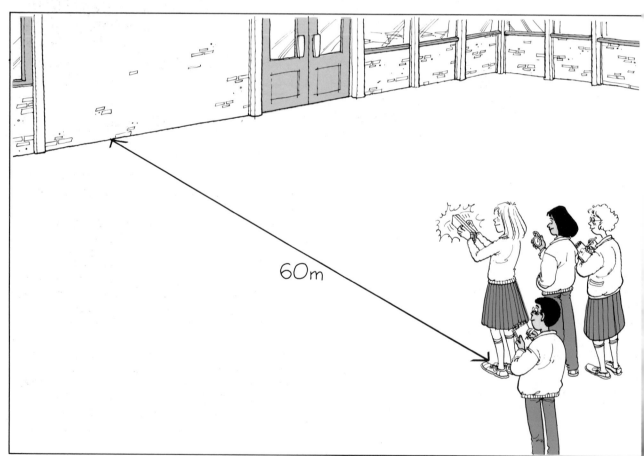

60m

Record

▶ Record how far the sound had moved by the time it came back to the group.

Getting an accurate answer

It seemed to take less than one second for the sound to get to the wall and come back again. This was such a short time that it was difficult for Wendy's group to time it carefully. They decided to try another **investigation**.

They clapped once, as before, and listened for the echo. Then they clapped a second time, just as they heard the first echo. They carried on clapping at the same time as they heard each echo. When they had built up a rhythm they timed twenty claps.

Plan

Try their investigation for yourselves.

Find something suitable for making loud claps.

Measure your distance *accurately* from a wall (it need not be exactly 60 metres).

Interpreting your results

After timing twenty claps, Wendy worked out that this was the time taken for the sound to go to the wall and back again twenty times. This was her **interpretation** of her measurements. Here is part of Wendy's notebook showing her results and her working out. Your result will probably not be exactly the same but it should be near. If it is very different (more than 400 metres per second or less than 200 metres per second) then you should check your results and working out. Did you remember to use your own distance from the wall in your calculations?

> We did the investigation 3 times, to check our results.
>
> | Go | Time for 20 Claps |
> |----|-------------------|
> | 1 | 7.5 seconds |
> | 2 | 8.5 seconds |
> | 3 | 8 seconds |
>
> We took an average of these 3 results:
> 7.5 + 8.5 + 8 = 24   24 ÷ 3 = 8 seconds
> For 1 clap the sound must have gone 60m × 2 (distance there and back) = 120 M.
> For 20 claps the sound must have gone 120 M × 20 = 2400M.
> So sound travelled 2400 M in 8 seconds.
> In 1 second it will go 2400 ÷ 8 = 300 M.
> So the speed of sound = 300 M/s.

Record

► Keep a record of your results.
▸ Add your results to a class chart.
▸ Compare your result with the results of the other groups.

You use speech to communicate with other people. You discuss your ideas with friends. You give each other advice and information. You probably argue with each other at times! You do all these things by speaking.

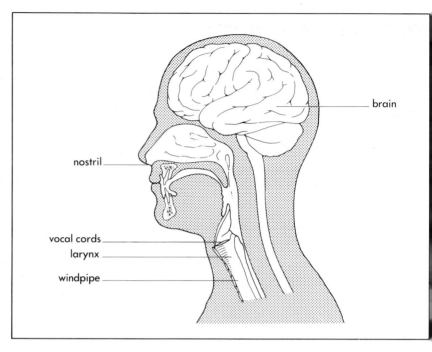

Discuss

▶ How do you think you make all the different sounds that other people recognize as speech? You are making some **inferences**.

One way that we can make different sounds is by controlling our 'vocal cords'. These are shown in the diagram above.

Record

▶ Do the exercise on Cut Out CM5 (part 1).

Making different sounds

Most mammals have vocal cords with which they make sounds. But humans can also shape their mouths to form different sounds. Our lips and tongues can be moved and shaped to produce the many different sounds of speech.

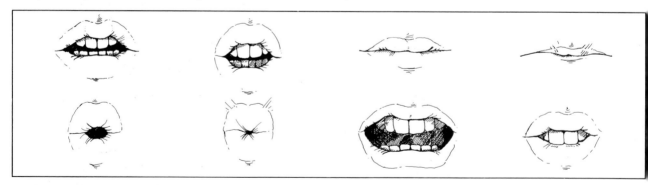

Discuss

Look at these pictures of lip shapes.
▶ **Predict** what sound each of these lip shapes will make?
▶ How could you check your predictions? When you do this you will be **experimenting**.
▶ How else do we make sounds to communicate?

Developing speech

Most children start talking at about the age of two. We know this from **observations** made of children all over the world. Children start to talk at about the same age, whatever the language they are learning and however they live. Because of this, scientists believe that people are born with the ability to learn to speak and that this is usually fully formed by the time they are two. This is a **hypothesis**.

The diagrams 1 – 6 show some of the stages children go through as they grow. Part 2 of Cut Out CM5 gives some of the stages of learning to talk.

1. Lifts head. Cannot grasp.
2. Stands with help.
3. Crawls.
4. Walks.
5. Walks upstairs.
6. Rides a tricycle.

Discuss

► Decide in your group which of the stages of learning to talk described on the Cut Out goes with each of the diagrams.

Record

► Cut out the sentences and put them into your book in the order you have decided on.
► Write a paragraph about each of these stages. Look at books on child development in the library or in the Health Education department.

Rates of development

Children develop at different rates. These graphs were made from observations of 100 different children.

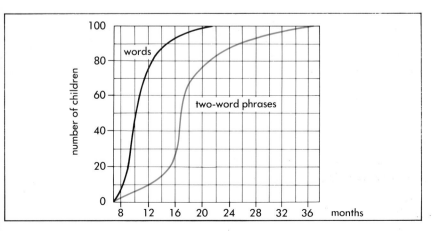

Record

► Write down the age when 60 of the children could say a two-word phrase.
► Write down the age when every child could say one word. These are your **interpretations**.
► Suggest who would use a graph like this. You are making an **inference**.

Telephones

Telephones are a very useful way of sending messages. Your school has telephones, offices and shops have telephones, you may have a telephone at home.

Discuss

► Discuss how often the people in your group use the telephone.
► What are the advantages of sending messages by telephone?
► When would you use a telephone rather than send a message by another means?

Making a telephone

A telephone can transfer sounds from one place to another. You can make your own very simple telephone.

Plan

You can try using lots of different materials. Discuss in your group what you are going to use. These will be your **investigations**.

◆ Is it best to use thick or thin string? What about wire or cotton?
◆ What makes the best mouthpiece? Try yoghurt pots or polystyrene cups or something else.
◆ What makes the best receiver? Try using the same things as for the mouthpiece.
◆ Does the size of the receiver make a difference?
◆ Does the size of the mouthpiece make a difference?
◆ Does the length of the string (or wire) between them make a difference?

When you answer these questions you will be making **interpretations**. Use your findings to design the best telephone. You will be **applying** what you know.

Record

► Make a record of what you and your group have done. You could make a table.
► Describe the best system you tried. Record what materials were used and whether this was the most expensive system.
▷ Try to make a tape recording of a short piece of speech using your best string telephone. Put the microphone at the receiving end of your telephone and speak into the mouthpiece.

Plan

Some pupils made the following two **predictions** about string telephones. Plan ways to test these predictions. You will be doing **experiments**.

'The telephone will not work when the string is slack'.

'The telephone will not work round corners'.

Record

- ▶ Record the two predictions.
- ▶ Say whether the results of your tests agree or disagree with the predictions. You will be **interpreting** your results.
- ▶ Record what you have found out about the way sound travels.

Present

- ▶ Make a large poster to advertise your telephone system. Remember to say what advantages your telephone has over other telephone systems.

Plan

Here are two more **investigations** for you to try.
- ▶ Can you extend your telephone system so that three or more people can hold a conversation together?
- ▶ Can you make a 'telephone exchange' so that different people can hold different conversations?

Ultrasound

Discuss

▶ In your group make a list of things you have heard said about bats, or seen in films or on television.
▶ Decide with which of these things you agree.

What is a bat?

Bats are a group of mammals that can fly. There are lots of different types of bat around the world. Some eat fish, some eat frogs and some eat fruit. All the types of bat in Britain eat insects. Bats can be helpful to people because many of the insects they eat are a nuisance to us. For example, bats eat woodworm insects in lofts.

Hunting insects

Bats normally hunt at night. They make very high-pitched sounds, either in their throats or in their noses. High pitched sound is called 'ultrasound'. Bats send pulses of ultrasound and then use the echoes to tell them if there are any insects flying nearby. They also use this system to avoid flying into walls or trees in the dark.

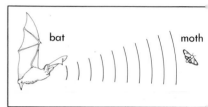

A bat sends out pulses of sound.

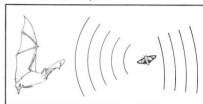

Part of each pulse is reflected back to the bat.

Record

Bats do not all hunt in the same way. Some bats fly quickly and catch insects in the air. Others hover above slow-moving insects on leaves or walls. The photographs below show two different bats. There are some statements about these two types of bat on Cut Out CM6.
▶ Cut out the statements and line drawings and arrange them into two groups under the drawing of each bat.

This bat has large ears which can detect very soft sounds. This bat does not fly very quickly (if it did, its large ears would slow it down).

This bat has small ears which are not very sensitive. However, it can fly quickly over open ground.

at detectors

The ultrasound that bats use is too high-pitched for most people to hear. Bats usually fly in darkness so it is difficult to study their behaviour. However, recently bat detectors have been developed. They are about the size of a pocket radio. They detect ultrasound and turn it into sound that people can hear. This has made it much easier to study bats.

Bats in London

The most common British bat is called the pipistrelle. Pipistrelles have been found living in all of the London parks below except for Green Park.

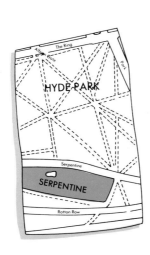

Discuss

- Discuss the maps above in your group. Talk about any differences you **observe** between Green Park and the other parks.
- Can you suggest why pipistrelles do not live in Green Park but do live in all the other parks shown here? This will be your **hypothesis**.

Record

- Make a record of all the hypotheses which your group suggested.
- Can you think of any places near your home or school where pipestrelles might live?

ibernation

here are not many insects or bats to eat in winter. Most bats in Britain 'hibernate' in the winter months. This means they go into a deep sleep. If they are woken they will fly away, using up energy that they cannot replace with food. For this reason bats should not be disturbed in winter.

Present

A neighbour is going to knock down an old shed on an allotment during the Christmas holidays. There may be bats in the shed.

- Write a letter trying to persuade your neighbour not to knock the shed down.

Discuss

- Look back to the list you made at the start of this activity. Have you changed your mind about any of these things?

Whale talk

Whales are large mammals which live in sea water. They often move around in groups called 'schools'. It is not usually possible to see much more than about 50 metres away, even in very clear water. Whales keep in contact with each other by producing low pitched sounds which can travel a long way in sea water. Some types of whale, such as the humpback whale, can communicate with other whales over 100 km away. Recordings of whale sounds (or 'songs' as they are called) have been made. The sounds sometimes last for 10 or 20 minutes without a break. This means that a whale probably sends quite a long message when it communicates to other whales. This is more like sending a letter than having a conversation!

Breaching

Whales are often seen leaping out of the water. This is very spectacular to watch and is known as 'breaching'. However not all types of whale breach. This **observation** led people to ask 'Why do whales breach at all?'

Discuss

Imagine your group is a school of whales!
► If you wanted to send a message to the other whales how would you make certain that they heard the complete message?
► What sort of things would you put in your message?

A humpback whale breaching.

Discuss

► Suggest some ideas which might explain why whales breach. You will be making **hypotheses**.

Type of whale	Do they live in groups or by themselves?	Length	Shape	Breaching rate
Blue	by themselves	45 m	thin	rare
Bowhead	unknown	25 m	medium	occasional
Bryde's	unknown	20 m	thin	occasional
Finback	by themselves	30 m	thin	rare
Grey	groups	15 m	round	often
Humpback	groups	15 m	round	often
Minke	unknown	9 m	round	rare
Right	groups	17 m	round	often
Sei	by themselves	18 m	thin	rare
Sperm	groups	30 m	round	often

ese **observations** and **measurements** were made by scientists who were trying to find out why whales breach.

Discuss

► Read the information in the table above and decide in your group which of the hypotheses opposite fit with it. You are **interpreting** the information in the table.
► Are these hypotheses the same as the ones you thought of in your group? Did you think of any others?

Some hypotheses

Whales breach in order to communicate.
Whales that live in groups will breach more often than whales that live by themselves.

Whales breach so that they can dive more deeply.
Round whales will breach more often than thin whales because their round shape is not so good for diving.

Whales breach to keep their backbone supple.
Long whales will breach more often than short whales.

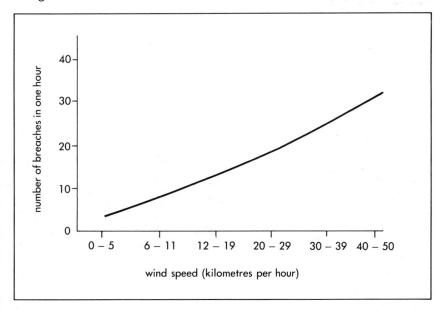

Discuss

Study the graph about breaching rate and wind speed.
  Do windy conditions affect breaching rate? How do you think windy conditions would affect the sea? Does the data from the graph support your hypothesis? Does it support any of the hypotheses above? You are **interpreting** the information in the graph.

Record

► Write down the hypothesis which your group think is most likely to be correct.
► Write down all the pieces of information which helped you to decide that this is the most likely explanation.

Why birds sing

Discuss

▶ Why do you think birds sing?
Look at the pictures on this page of birds singing.
▶ How do you think they are using their song?
▶ What effect do you think their song is having? You are making **inferences**.

Protecting territory

A territorial bird song is one which a bird may sing to keep other birds out of its area, or territory. This is like a person putting up a 'KEEP OUT' or 'NO TRESPASSERS' sign. A group of scientists were studying this type of bird song. They made this **prediction**:

'A bird will sing more if it hears the territorial song of another bird'.

Discuss

▶ Do you agree with their prediction?

Testing the prediction

The scientists wanted to test their predictions. They did the following **experiment**.

First they found a number of birds of the same type and recorded some of their songs on tape. Then they listened to a 'test' bird (a bird they had chosen to study) for five minutes and wrote down how many times it sang during this time.

They had already recorded the song of a neighbouring bird of the same type. They immediately played this recording to the test bird for five minutes. They wrote down how many times it sang during these five minutes.

Finally they switched off the tape recorder and wrote down how many times the test bird sang in the next five minutes.

Later they did the same experiment again using the same test bird but a recording of another bird from a *different wood*. The scientists noted all their **observations** and measurements on graphs.

Discuss

Look at the graphs.
► Did the test bird sing before the recording was played?
► How did playing the tape recording affect the number of songs it sang?
► Which tape recording made more difference to the number of songs it sang?
► What happened to the number of songs when the tape recording was turned off in each case? You have been **interpreting** the graphs.
► Do you think the results agree with the scientists' prediction?
► Why do you think the scientists observed the birds for five minutes before switching on the tape?
► The scientists tested a lot more birds. Why could they not rely on just this one set of results? You are making some **inferences**.

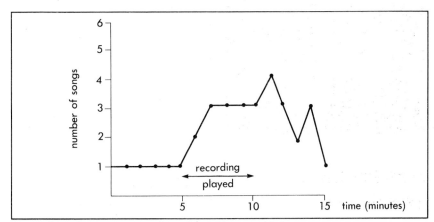

Song of test bird using recording of neighbouring bird.

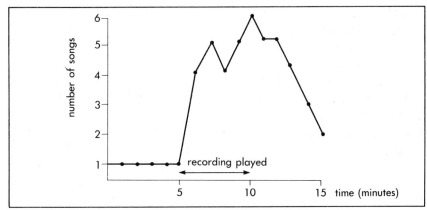

Song of test bird using recording of bird from different wood.

Present

► Imagine that you and your group are the scientists who carried out this experiment. Write or make a recording of an account of the experiment for your open evening at school. Describe in your account how you did the complete experiment and any problems you had in getting your results.

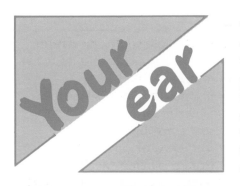

Your ear

The ear is the sense organ that makes us able to hear. It is made up of many delicate parts. Most of these parts are inside the skull where they are protected. This means that you cannot usually see them. Only one part of the ear can be seen easily.

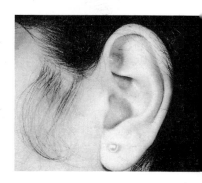

Discuss

▶ Look closely at the diagram below and then read Cut Out CM7 (part 1).
▶ Decide in your group which **observation** matches each part of the ear. (These observations were made by examining an ear very carefully.)

Record

▶ Stick the diagram of the ear from Cut Out CM7 into your workbook.
▶ Label the diagram with the labels and the matching observations given in the Cut Out.
▶ Read the sentences in part 2 of the Cut Out. These are **inferences**. Arrange these in an order which best describes how the ear works.
▶ Shade with dots the parts of the diagram that are *filled with air*.
▶ Choose one colour and use this to shade in all the *bones*.
▶ Choose a second colour to shade in all the *skin*.
▶ Choose a third colour to shade in all the *tubes in which there is liquid*.
▶ Choose a fourth colour to shade in the *nerve*.
▶ Make a key to show what each colour means.

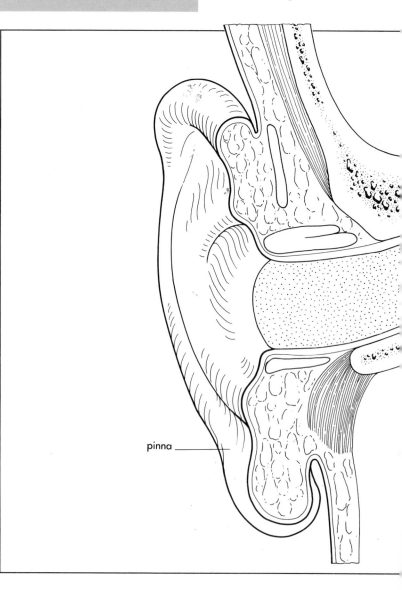

pinna

Observations

A coiled tube.

A nerve which goes from the ear to the brain.

A thin piece of skin.

A tube joining the throat and ear.

The large flap of the ear that you can see.

The bones that are between the ear drum and the tubes filled with liquid.

Three half circles joined together.

Inferences

These are arranged to sense movement in any direction.

This carries messages to the brain.

This changes movements in the liquid into messages for the brain.

This collects sound waves.

This stops your ears 'popping' by letting air move between the ear and the throat.

These bones carry the vibration from the ear drum to the liquid.

This is vibrated by sound waves.

Present

▶ Match each of the observations above to the correct inference listed above and make a chart to record your arrangement.

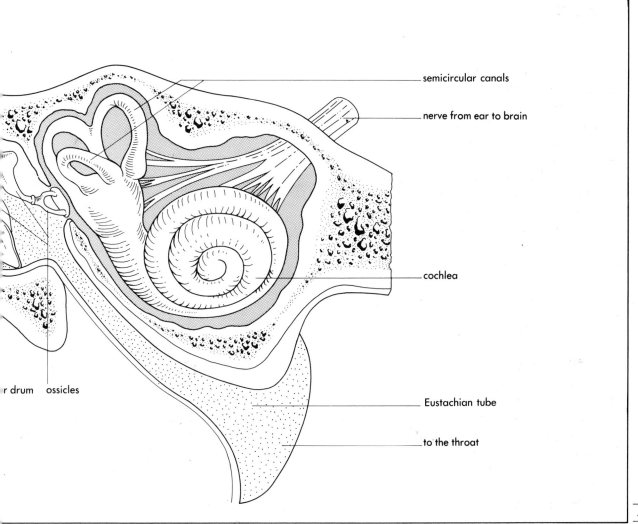

semicircular canals

nerve from ear to brain

cochlea

ear drum   ossicles

Eustachian tube

to the throat

Communication
— some useful words

advertise
aerial
alarm
amplifier
animal
audio
book
broadcast
cables
car
CB
cell-net
cipher
code
colour
communicate
computer
data
ear
error
exchange
expression
eye
fire
flag
frequency
hear
heliograph
hormone
indicator
information
intercept

interference
language
laser
letter
light
listen
lorry
loudhailer
magazine
medium
message
microwave
newspaper
noise
optic fibres
pipes
post
public address
radar
radio
railway
receive
report
road
rumour
running
satellite
semaphore
sensory
SETI
shout
sight

sign
signal
smell
smoke
song
sound
speak
speech
speed
stage-coach
talk
taste
teleconference
telegram
telegraph
telephone
telescope
television
tell
terminal
touch
traffic light
transmit
ultrasound
vibration
video
visual
voice
whisper
wires
word

Time

Contents

Candles	5.1
Corrosion	5.2
Cotton reel tractors	5.3
Dating	5.4
Extinction	5.5
Human timers	5.6
Ideas about the universe	5.7
Lines of time	5.8
The night sky	5.9
Planets	5.10
Rocks	5.11
The Sun	5.12
Swinging	5.13
Timers	5.14
Timing chemical reactions	5.15
Time – some useful words	5.16

Symbols you will find:

These are things you should try to do.

These are extra things to do if you have time.

These are questions to think about when you are planning practical work.

When you see this symbol you need to take extra care.

This theme contains 15 spreads which can be worked through in any order.

Theme 5

Candles

Discuss

► What do you think is happening in the photograph?
  You are **interpreting** the photograph.
► When do you use candles?
► How do you think they are made?

Candles as timing devices

Plan

⚠ Make a timing device from a candle.

♦ What sort of candle will you use?
♦ How long will it burn?
♦ What units of time will your candle timer measure?
♦ How will you fix it upright so that it does not fall over?
♦ How will you make regular marks on the candle, so that you can see how far it has burned?

♦ How far apart will the marks be on the candle?

Try a number of different candles. **Predict** how quickly you think each candle will burn.

Record

Veronica's group made charts of their results like this.
► Make similar charts of your results.

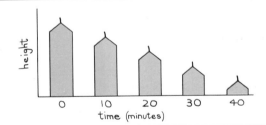

Discuss

► Which of your results agree with your predictions?

Plan

► Try using the weight lost from the candle (instead of the height) as a measure of time.

How long do candles burn?

Plan

In this activity you are going to find out how long a
candle flame stays alight. You will be doing an **investigation**.

Fix a candle to a dish.
◆ What different things happen when you
cover the candle with a jar?

◆ What happens when you cover the flame
with different pieces of glassware? Make
as many **observations** as you can.

Discuss

Paul's group had the idea that the taller
the jar, the longer the candle will burn.
▶ Do your results agree with this
hypothesis?
▶ Can you think of other things which
affect how quickly candles burn?

▶ Arrange your pieces of glassware in
order of how much air you think they
hold. You are making **inferences**.
▶ How could you check your inferences?
(Ask your teacher for help if you
need to.)

Record

▶ Make a table of your results. Write
down Paul's group's hypothesis.

▶ Complete this sentence: We (agree/
disagree) with Paul's group because ...

Plan

You have already discussed some of the things you know
about candles. Now carry out an **investigation** to find out
more. You may need to look in the school library or ask
other members of your class how they use candles.

Present

▶ Make a poster to show
your findings.

5.1

Corrosion

Do you know what a rodent is? It is an animal that gnaws at things. The name comes from a Latin word *rodere*, meaning 'to gnaw'.

The word 'corrode' comes from the same Latin word. You can use it to describe the effect of chemicals on some metals. Corrosion means that something is being steadily 'gnawed' or 'eaten away'. Over a period of time many metals become badly corroded by chemicals in the air.

Bronze age jewellery

Discuss

▶ Where have you seen metal corrosion?
▶ Why do some things corrode more quickly than others?
▶ How can you slow down the rate at which things corrode?

Plan

In this activity you are going to look at the effect of air on metals. You will be **investigating**.

Clean half of each strip of metal. When you have cleaned the pieces, put them back in the Petri dish and leave them for at least a week.

◆ Are all the pieces shiny after cleaning?
◆ Are they still shiny after a week? (You could clean one piece and compare the rest.)
◆ How has the colour changed?

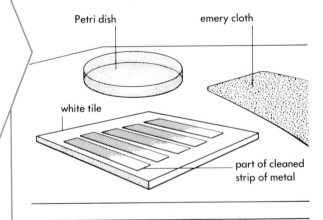

Record

▶ Make a 'before and after' table to show any changes you **observed**.

Discuss

▶ After doing this Wayne's group suggested that 'air corrodes metals'. This was their **hypothesis**. How could you test it?

Plan

Rusting is another kind of corrosion. Find out about it using the apparatus below. This will be your **investigation**

Set up these test tubes and leave them for a week.

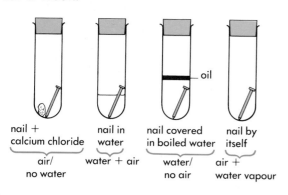

nail + calcium chloride	nail in water	nail covered in boiled water	nail by itself
air/ no water	water + air	water/ no air	air + water vapour

Record

▶ Wayne's group made this table of their results. Make a similar table.

TUBE	RUSTY OR NOT	WAS AIR PRESENT?	WAS WATER PRESENT?
1			
2			
3			
4			

Discuss

▶ What conditions are needed for nails to rust?
Wayne's group thought 'If we can stop air and water getting to a nail, we can stop it rusting'. This was their **prediction**. They suggested using paint or vaseline to stop the rust.
▶ How could you test their prediction? You could try out your **experiment**.

Plan

Many metals are quickly corroded by acids. Magnesium is one of these. Find out what effect acid has on magnesium.

Make three different concentrations of acid.

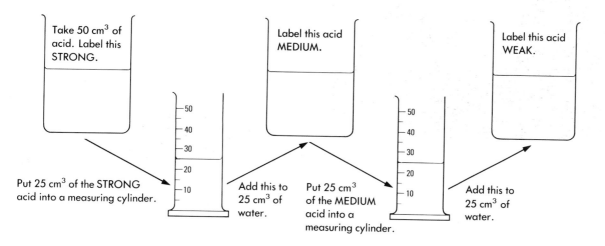

Take 50 cm³ of acid. Label this STRONG.

Put 25 cm³ of the STRONG acid into a measuring cylinder.

Add this to 25 cm³ of water.

Label this acid MEDIUM.

Put 25 cm³ of the MEDIUM acid into a measuring cylinder.

Add this to 25 cm³ of water.

Label this acid WEAK.

◆ How long does it take for a piece of magnesium to disappear in each concentration of acid?
◆ Was this a fair test? **Evaluate** your test.

Observe what happens with other metals.
◆ Can you find a pattern in your results? You are **interpreting** your results.

Follow the plan

Follow the steps for making a cotton reel tractor.
Make one each so that you can race them.

⚠ Cut a piece of candle so that the length of the reel and the candle piece is about the same as the length of the rubber band.

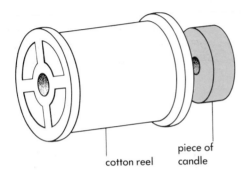

cotton reel   piece of candle

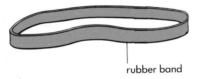

rubber band

The candle piece will have a hole where the wick was. Use a needle or matchstick to make the hole large enough for the rubber band.

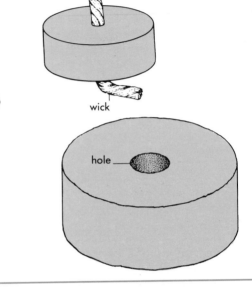

wick

hole

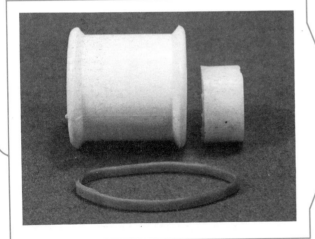

Record

▶ Make a record of the results of several races.
▶ Record how far your cotton reel tractor moved in ten seconds.
▶ Work out the speed of your tractor in centimetres per second (cm/s). To do this you will need to divide your previous answer by ten.

Discuss

None of the tractors made by you and your group will be exactly the same. Some will go faster, some will go further, some may be better at climbing over objects.

▶ What part of the cotton reel tractor design causes these differences? You are making an **inference**.
▶ How could you use your tractor as a timing device?

Thread the rubber band through the centre of the candle piece and the cotton reel. Forceps (tweezers) or a bent needle may help to pull the band through.

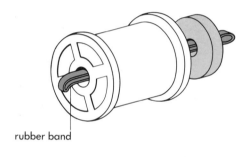

rubber band

Push a short matchstick or wire clip through one end of the rubber band. Push a full length matchstick through the candle end. Decorate your tractor. Design a suitable racing course for your tractor.

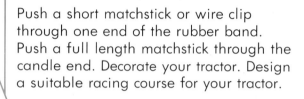

wire clip   matchstick

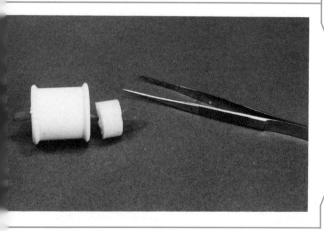

◆ How does the tractor move along a flat surface when it is wound up?
◆ What is the biggest object it can climb over? Make some **observations**.

Plan

▶ You now have some ideas about how to design a cotton reel tractor. **Apply** these ideas to design a cotton reel tractor that will go further than any you have made before.

Present

▶ Make a class chart of your results.

Dating

Discuss

Look at the four pictures below.
► Put them in an order starting with the one you think is oldest.
► What clues in the pictures suggest the date of the scene? You will be **inferring**.

Tree ring dating

Archaeologists study history by looking at ancient remains. They often need to know how old things are. For example, they may dig up samples of wood. They can date this wood by **applying** their knowledge of how trees grow.

Every year in the life of a live tree, a new layer is added to its trunk and branches. This means that the younger layers are towards the outside and the older layers are in the middle of the trunk. If the tree is cut down you can see these layers as a series of rings. By counting the number of rings you can discover the age of the tree.

Discuss

► How old were the trees in the picture on the right when they were cut down?

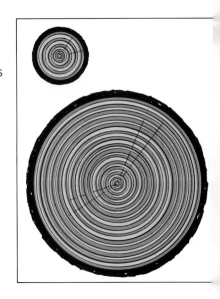

In Britain, trees do most of their growing in the spring. This seasonal growth makes the rings easy to see. In some countries, trees grow throughout the year, so the rings are more difficult to see.

Tree rings do not just tell you the age of the tree. They also tell you when a tree grew well because the weather was warm and there was plenty of rain, or when it grew badly, because of cold or drought. This means we can **infer** what the weather was like in the past.

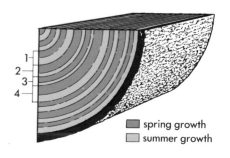

1
2
3
4

■ spring growth
□ summer growth

Record

▶ Copy the diagram above and label it with the likely climate for years 1 – 4.

tree A

tree B

Discuss

▶ Where do you see the older rings on a sawn tree trunk?
▶ How can you tell that tree B started growing before tree A?
▶ Do the dating exercise on Cut Out TM1 (part 1).

Pollen analysis

Another way of dating things is by examining pollen. Most plants produce lots of pollen in their flowers. Pollen is very small (you need a microscope to see it properly) and very tough. It lasts a long time in mud and dirt. People can work out how old mud is by looking at the pollen in it. Archaeologists have found pollen that may be 12 000 years old.

Record

▶ Do Cut Out TM1 (part 2) to find out how pollen analysis works.

This body was found in a peat bog in 1984. After looking at the pollen from the surrounding peat, archaeologists **inferred** *that it was about 2300 years old.*

Extinction

Too late

What is 'extinction'? When the last one of a particular plant or animal dies, and there are none left, the animal or plant is 'extinct'.

Below are two animals that have become extinct in the last 500 years, the dodo and the Tasmanian wolf. They are extinct because of the actions of human beings.

Dodo

Tasmanian wolf

Discuss

▶ What do you think people did to make these animals extinct? One idea is that they died out because people destroyed the places where they lived. This is one **hypothesis**, which may be right or wrong. Think of some more hypotheses.

Fossils

Species become extinct in other ways. Many millions of animals and plants died out before people existed on the Earth. People only know about these because of 'fossils'. A fossil is the remains of an animal or plant which has been preserved in rock. By studying fossils, scientists can estimate the dates when living things were alive and when they became extinct.

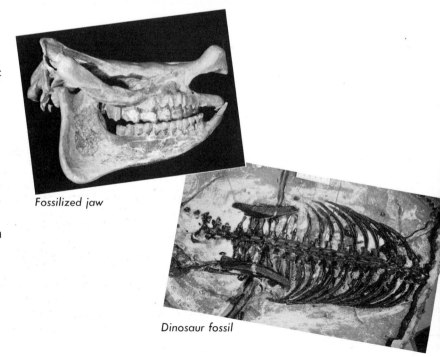

Fossilized jaw

Dinosaur fossil

Information from fossils has been used to make this table.

Name	Group	150	125	100	75	50	25	0(now)
Carnivora (meat-eaters)	Mammal					✓	✓	✓
Chelonia (turtles)	Reptile	✓	✓	✓	✓	✓	✓	✓
Chiroptera (bats)	Mammal					✓	✓	✓
Insectivora (insect-eaters)	Mammal					✓	✓	✓
Neognathae (new-jawed)	Bird					✓	✓	✓
Odonthognathae (serrated-billed)	Bird	✓	✓	✓	✓			
Ornithischia (bird-hipped)	Reptile	✓	✓	✓	✓			
Pterosaurs (flying dinosaurs)	Reptile	✓	✓	✓	✓			
Primates (apes and monkeys)	Mammal					✓	✓	✓
Rodents (rats)	Mammal					✓	✓	✓
Sauropoda (lizard-footed)	Reptile	✓	✓	✓	✓			
Taeniodont (tube-toothed)	Mammal					✓		
Theropoda (warm-footed)	Reptile	✓	✓	✓	✓			

Millions of years ago

✓ = Known to exist at the time.

The table shows that between 75 and 50 million years ago, there was an enormous change in the type of animals living on the Earth. This period is sometimes called the 'Great Extinction'.

Discuss

▶ Why is this period called the 'Great Extinction'?
▶ What do you think happened to the birds at the time of the 'Great Extinction'?
You are making **inferences**.

Record

▶ Use the table to complete the sentences below.
The animals which are now extinct are the ...
There were no bats or primates on the Earth before ...
One type of mammal that is now extinct is ...
A reptile that existed 150 million years ago and is still found today is the ...

Time is running out

Many types of animals and plants will die out unless they are protected. These are called 'endangered species'. The Bengal tiger is an example.

Present

▶ Find out why some species are now endangered.
▶ How can people prevent this happening?
▶ Prepare a leaflet telling people about endangered species and how they can be protected.

Bengal tiger

Human timers

Your heart pumps blood around your body. In some of the parts of your body where the blood runs near the surface you can feel the pumping. This regular pumping is called a 'pulse'.

Discuss

► Who usually takes your pulse?
► What information do you think your pulse can give?
► What might alter your pulse rate?
► Could you use your pulse as a timing device?

Plan

Find out about your pulse rate and how it varies. You will be doing an **investigation**.
Start by making sure you can take your pulse rate. Use the photographs to help you find places where you can find your pulse easily.

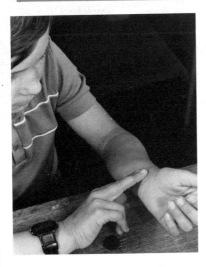
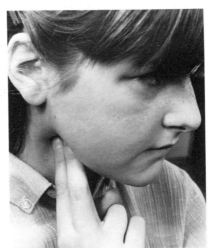
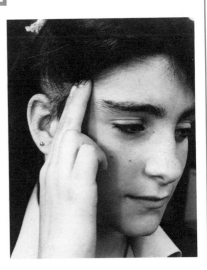

Time your pulse rate when you are in different positions.
◆ What different positions will you choose?
Time your pulse rate before and after exercise.
◆ What sort of exercise will you do?
◆ How long does it take your pulse rate to return to its 'before exercise' rate?

Try using other body rates (e.g. breathing or blinking) as timing devices.
◆ Are they more or less useful than pulse rates?

Discuss

► Are your results the same as those of other people in your group?
► If they are different, suggest a reason for this. You will be making an **inference**.

Record

► Make records of your results. You could use bar graphs.
► Make a report on what you have done and what you have found out.

Timing reactions

Nisha was testing reaction times. She held a ruler above Ben's hand so that his thumb was in line with the 0 cm mark. When she dropped the ruler Ben had to catch it. She could see how quickly he reacted by checking the point where his hand had grabbed the ruler. This was her **investigation**.

After collecting quite a lot of results Nisha thought she had found a pattern. She thought 'the more often people do this the quicker they get.' This was her **hypothesis**.

Plan

Try Nisha's investigation yourself.
- Do the results in your group agree with Nisha's hypothesis?
- What else affects reaction times?
- Can you design a better reaction timer?

Record

▶ Describe what you did and what you found out.

Another way of timing reactions

A computer can easily be converted into a reaction timer. This program works for RML 380Z and 480Z computers.

Plan

▶ Test this reaction timer.
- Do the results agree with the investigation above?

```
10 PRINT "Wait ..."
20 FOR I=1 to RND(1)*1000
30 NEXT I
40 PRINT "Press the SPACE BAR."
50 K=GET(1000)
60 T=(1000-GET(-2))/1000
70 PRINT T;" seconds"
80 GOTO 10
```

Ideas about the universe

Have you ever wondered about the universe, how it is made up and how it was formed? There are many ideas about the universe, and they are changing and developing all the time.

Here are two ideas about the Earth.

The Earth is flat, like a piece of paper.

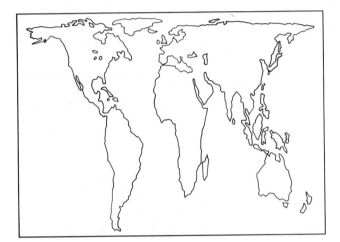

The Earth is round, like a ball.

Plan

Models may help you understand these ideas.

Try making models of your own. This group is using plasticine and wire to make models.
◆ What materials will you use?

Discuss

▶ Look at the **observations** on Cut Out TM2.
▶ Which observations support the 'flat Earth' idea?
▶ Which observations support the 'round Earth' idea?
▶ Can you think of some other pieces of evidence to support either idea?
▶ Which observations support *both* ideas?
▶ Which observations do not support *either* idea?

Here are two more ideas.

The Earth goes round the Sun.

The Sun goes round the Earth.

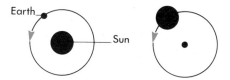

Earth — Sun

Discuss

▶ Look at the observations on Cut Out TM2.
▶ Which observations support the idea of the Sun moving?

▶ Which observations support the idea of the Earth moving?
▶ Which observations support *both* ideas?

In the last hundred years or so astronomers have been able to gain more information than ever before, using modern telescopes and other instruments. They have discovered many millions of stars, and raised more **questions** about the universe.

Here are two recent ideas about the universe.

New stars are being made all the time. New stars replace old stars so there are always about the same number. This **hypothesis** *is part of the Steady State Theory.*

The universe began with an enormous explosion 13.5 billion years ago. All the stars were formed then. The universe is still expanding. This **hypothesis** *is part of the Big Bang Theory.*

Plan

You can find out more about the Big Bang Theory by making a model of it with a balloon. You will be doing an **investigation**.

Put some marks on the balloon. These represent the stars.

Blow up the balloon.

Discuss

▶ The model of the expanding universe suggests that stars should be moving away from each other all the time. Does your model show this?
▶ Astronomers have noticed that the further stars are from the Earth, the closer they are to each other. This is an **observation**. Does it support either of the theories?

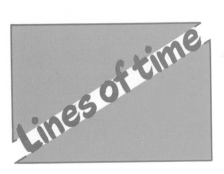

Lines of time

The top line represents time from the beginning of the universe to the present day. The second line is a magnification of the end of the first line and shows the most recent thousand million years. The third line is a magnification of a tiny part of the second line and shows the most recent hundred million years. The fourth line is a magnification of a very tiny part of the third line and shows the most recent forty thousand years.

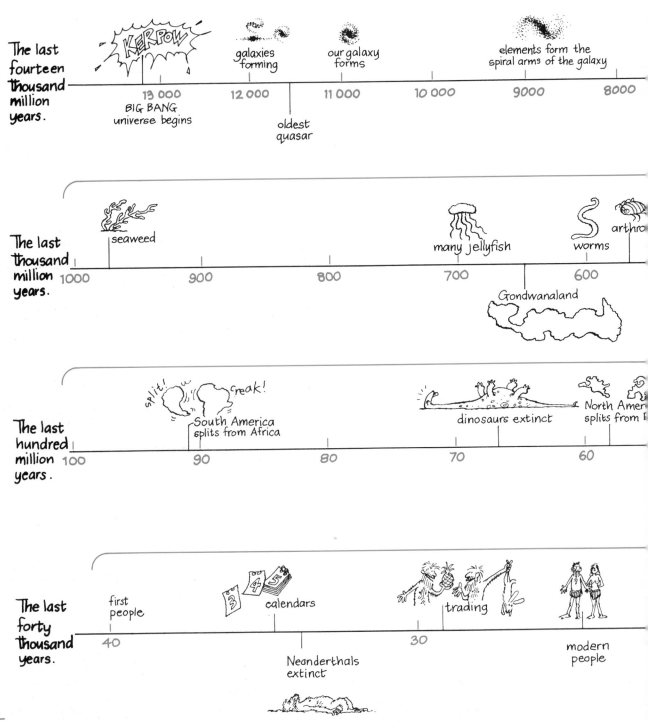

The last fourteen thousand million years.

galaxies forming	our galaxy forms			elements form the spiral arms of the galaxy	

13 000 BIG BANG universe begins   12 000   11 000   10 000   9000   8000

oldest quasar

The last thousand million years.

seaweed   many jellyfish   worms   arthro

1000   900   800   700   600

Gondwanaland

The last hundred million years.

split!   creak!   dinosaurs extinct   North Amer splits from E

South America splits from Africa

100   90   80   70   60

The last forty thousand years.

first people   calendars   trading

40   30

Neanderthals extinct

modern people

5.8

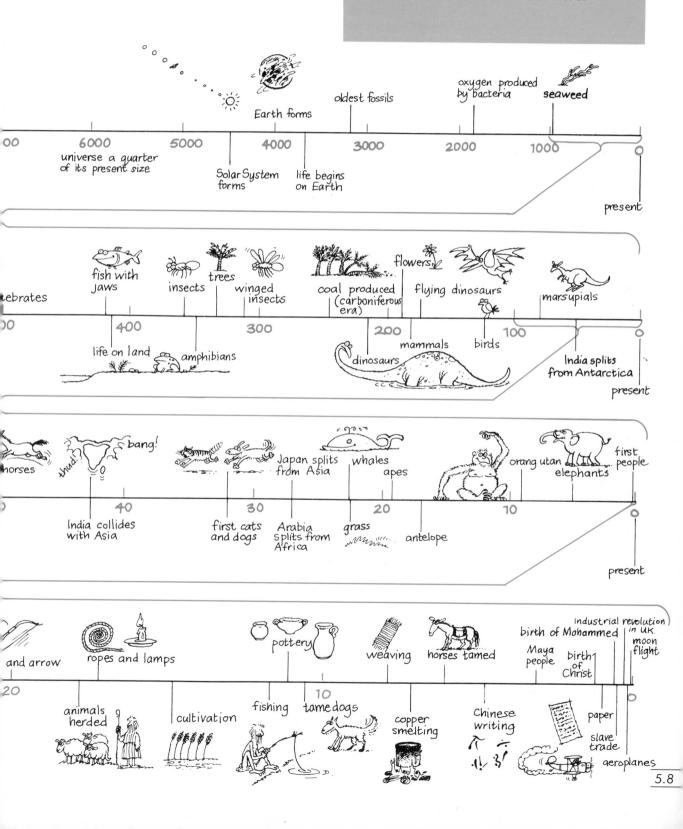

Present

► Make your own time line for the last ten years.
► Do the exercise on Cut Out TM 3.

oxygen produced by bacteria

seaweed

oldest fossils

Earth forms

| OO | 6000 | 5000 | 4000 | 3000 | 2000 | 1000 |

universe a quarter of its present size

Solar System forms

life begins on Earth

present

fish with jaws

insects

trees

winged insects

coal produced (carboniferous era)

flowers

flying dinosaurs

marsupials

ebrates

| OO | 400 | 300 | 200 | 100 |

life on land

amphibians

dinosaurs

mammals

birds

India splits from Antarctica

present

horses

thud?

bang!

Japan splits from Asia

whales

apes

orang utan

elephants

first people

| 40 | 30 | 20 | 10 |

India collides with Asia

first cats and dogs

Arabia splits from Africa

grass

antelope

present

and arrow

ropes and lamps

pottery

weaving

horses tamed

birth of Mohammed

Industrial revolution in U.K.

moon flight

Maya people

birth of Christ

| 20 | 10 | 0 |

animals herded

cultivation

fishing

tame dogs

copper smelting

Chinese writing

paper

slave trade

aeroplanes

5.8

The night sky

The changing patterns of the moon and stars have been used as a method of time-keeping for thousands of years.

Discuss

▶ Do the stars in the night sky always appear in the same place?
▶ What changes have you seen?
▶ What changes in the night sky have you seen in a week? These are your **observations**.

The two pictures below show the night sky that people in Britain see in summer and winter. The constellations are marked with lines. Constellations are groups of stars which are easy to recognize. Once you have found Cassiopeia in the sky, it is much easier to find the other stars.

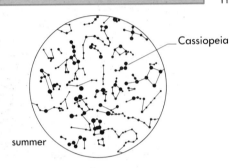

Cassiopeia

summer

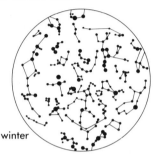

winter

Making a planisphere

Follow the plan

A planisphere is a map of the stars with a moveable mask. The mask shuts off some of the stars on the map. The stars which show are the ones you could see on a particular day. You could use your planisphere to find out what time of year it is but you probably know that already! If you know the date you can use the planisphere to **predict** which stars you should be able to see.

Cut out the two circles on Cut Out TM4. Cut out the inner section of circle B. Stick circle A onto stiff card. Stick circle B on to a piece of clear plastic.

Cut away any card or plastic outside the circles. Pin the two discs together so that B can move while A stays still.

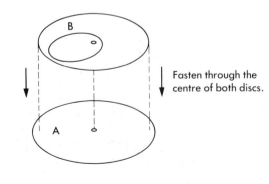

B

Fasten through the centre of both discs.

A

Using your planisphere

Follow the plan

How do you use your planisphere? Imagine that it is 1800 hours on 9th January.

Turn circle B until 1800 hours lines up with 9th January. The stars you would be able to see at this time are shown in the clear area.

To find out where they are in the sky, hold the planisphere above your head (make sure you can still see the map!) and point midnight on the mask towards North. You may need to use a compass to find North.

◆ At what times on 24th August and 8th October should you be able to see the same view of the sky as at 1800 hours on 9th January?

Present

▷ Draw a poster showing what stars you would be able to see from your classroom window at midnight tonight.

Making a telescope

Plan

A telescope is a useful instrument for observing the night sky. How can you make a telescope from two lenses? This will be your **investigation**.

◆ What happens if you change the distance between the lenses? This is your **observation**.
▷ Design a more permanent telescope in which the distance between the two lenses can be changed easily.

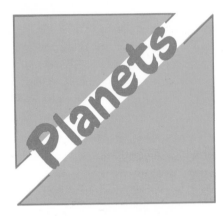

Planets

A year is the time it takes for the planet Earth to go once round the Sun. Other planets take different times to go round the Sun so their 'years' are different. A 'year' on Mars is about two Earth years. A 'year' on Jupiter is about 12 Earth years.

Discuss

▶ Which planets have 'years' longer than Earth's years? (Use the table opposite to help you.)

A day is the time it takes for the Earth to spin itself round once. Other planets take different times to spin round, so their days are different as well.

Discuss

▶ How many planets have longer 'days' than an Earth day? Do they have longer 'years' as well?

You are **interpreting** the information on the table.

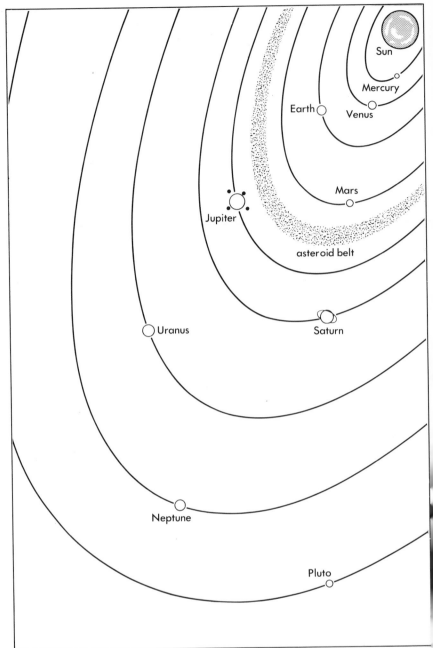

Here are some ideas about planets.

(a) Planets get cooler the further they are away from the Sun.

(b) The larger the planet the more moons it has.

(c) Planets further from the Sun have further to travel.

(d) Planets further from the Sun have longer 'years' because they travel more slowly.

Discuss

▶ Does the data in the table opposite support these **hypotheses**?

▶ There is only one planet that has liquid water on its surface. Suggest the reason for this.

This table gives you some information about the planets in the Solar System.

Name	Distance from Sun (million km)	Earth time to go once round the Sun	Diameter (km)	Number of moons	Earth time to spin round	Daytime surface temperature (°C)
Mercury	60	88 days	4 880	0	59 days	350
Venus	108	224 days	12 104	0	243 days	480
Earth	150	365 days/1 year	12 756	1	24 hours	22
Mars	228	2 years	6 787	2	24 hours	−23
Jupiter	778	12 years	142 200	16	10 hours	−150
Saturn	1 427	29 years	119 300	17	10 hours	−180
Uranus	2 870	84 years	51 800	14	23 hours	−210
Neptune	4 497	165 years	49 500	2	22 hours	−220
Pluto	5 900	248 years	3 000	1	6 days	−230

Record

▶ Do the exercise on Cut Out TM5 (part 1). Say where the imaginary planets will be 10 years and 20 years after the date in the diagrams on the Cut Out.
You will be **predicting**.

Planets get their name from the ancient Greek word 'planetos'. This word means 'a wanderer'. The ancient Greeks called planets wanderers because they appear to change position, wandering slowly through the stars.

The photograph shows the planet Mars 'wandering' against the background of stars. This picture was taken by photographing the same part of the sky on several nights in a row.

The diagrams below show how the planet Pluto moved between two nights. This is how Pluto was first discovered in 1930 — by looking at photographs taken on different nights.

Record

▶ Try the activity on Cut Out TM5 (part 2) and see if you can spot the planet.

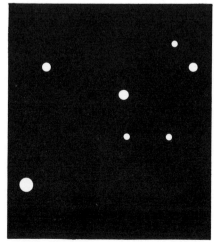

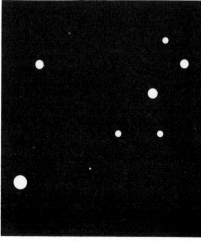

Rocks

The Earth is probably over four billion years old. During this time it has gone through many changes. The land you live on is made up of lots of different types of rock. These rocks have been made at different times and in different ways.

Layers of rock

People who study rocks and the Earth are called geologists. Geologists have noticed many things about the way the Earth is formed. They use their **observations** to make **inferences** about the history of the Earth. One important inference is that in layers of different rocks, the oldest ones will be at the bottom and the youngest ones will be at the top. This is a bit like filling a dustbin.

The rubbish you threw away first will be at the bottom of the dustbin and the rubbish you threw away last will be at the top.

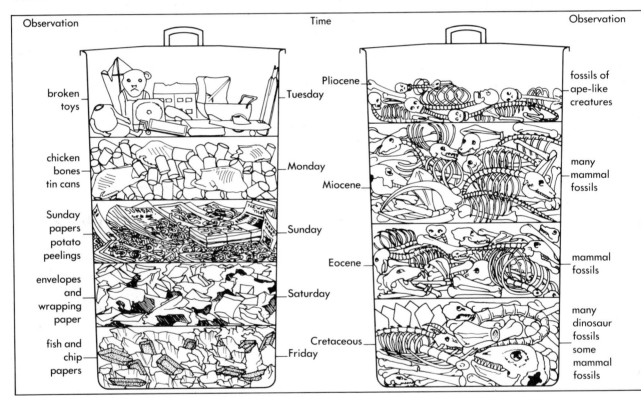

Record

▶ Use the information in the diagram to write a short account of what the owners of the dustbin did from Friday until Tuesday. You will be making **inferences**.
▶ Use the information to write a short account of what happened to life on Earth from the Cretaceous period until the Pliocene period. You will be making more **inferences**.
▶ Make a dustbin diagram of your own, showing what you have thrown away over a week. What **inferences** could be made from your diagram?

Seaside rocks

It is often easiest to see rock layers at the seaside where there are cliffs. This photograph was taken near Lulworth Cove in Dorset. The rocks in the photograph are:
Kimmeridge clay (139 million years old),
Portland stone (132 million years old), and
Portland clay (129 million years old).

Discuss

▶ Which rock do you think is which? You are **applying** what you know.

The rocks in the photograph are not in straight layers. They have been folded into a V shape. Geologists think that the rocks have been bent and buckled by strong sideways movements. This is an **inference**. You might find it hard to imagine land moving like this. But geologists think that *all* land is moving. This is their **hypothesis**.

This hypothesis is known as 'Continental Drift'. It says that the whole of the Earth's surface is made of huge plates, or rafts, which drift around very slowly. Sometimes they bump into each other. When this happens the huge force of the collision bends the rocks into new shapes.

Record

▶ Find out more about continental drift by doing Cut Out TM6.

Using geological knowledge

The map shows an island and the plants growing on it.

You can see the sequence of rocks in the area – coal is the bottom layer.

The key shows what type of rock the plants grow on.

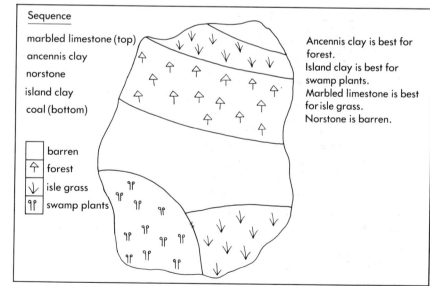

Sequence

marbled limestone (top)
ancennis clay
norstone
island clay
coal (bottom)

☐ barren
⬆ forest
⬇ isle grass
🌿 swamp plants

Ancennis clay is best for forest.
Island clay is best for swamp plants.
Marbled limestone is best for isle grass.
Norstone is barren.

Record

▶ Copy the map and label it with the type of rock that is nearest the surface in each area.
▶ Mark on your map a place where the coal could be mined most easily.
You are **interpreting** the information in the diagram.

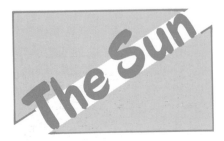

The Sun

Using the Sun as a clock

Discuss

▶ What happens to the shadow of a tree or tall building during a sunny day?
▶ How could you use shadows to tell the time?

Present

▶ The photograph shows a sundial. Design and make a simple sundial from card or wood.

Using the Sun as a calendar

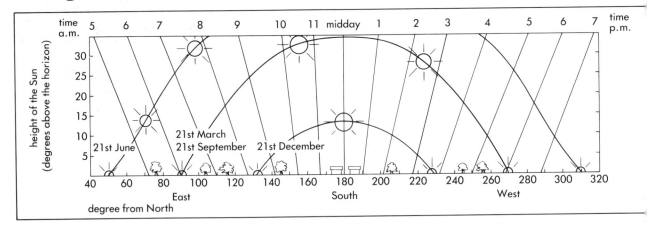

Discuss

The chart above shows the path of the Sun at different times of the year.

Follow the path of the Sun from sunrise to sunset on the shortest day of the year (21st December). Follow the Sun's path on 21st March. Follow the Sun's path on the longest day of the year (21st June), imagining the part which is not shown.

▶ How many hours can the Sun be seen in London on 21st December, 21st March, 21st June, and 21st September?
▶ About how many hours is the Sun in the sky on your birthday?

While you were doing this work you probably **observed** that the path of the Sun changes regularly.

People in early times **applied** their knowledge of the movement of the Sun to things like growing and harvesting crops. They used the Sun as a calendar.

Some built complicated circles of stone to help them observe and **predict** the movement of the Sun. The best known of these in Britain is Stonehenge.

Record

▶ Find out about Stonehenge and other stone circles.

Albertine's group decided to find out about the length of a shadow cast by a pole in the playground. They measured the shortest shadow made by the pole on the 21st day of each month. They missed August because of the holidays. They were very lucky with the weather during their **investigation**!

Here are their **observations**.

DATE	SHADOW LENGTH
21st Jan	16 m
21st Feb	10 m
21st March	9 m
21st April	5 m
21st May	3 m
21st June	2 m
21st July	3 m
21st Aug	—
21st Sept	7 m
21st Oct	10 m
21st Nov	16 m
21st Dec	20 m

Record

▶ Draw a graph of these results using Cut Out TM7.
▶ Use your graph to suggest what was the shortest shadow length in August.
  You are **interpreting** your graph.
▶ Make a sketch of what the graph would look like if the observations had been made over five years instead of one.
  You are **inferring**.
▶ Suggest what time of day you would see the shortest shadows.
▶ Explain why the measurements were always made on the same day of each month.

Swinging

Barry, Chung, Josette, and Shona were late for school.

They had been playing on the swing in the park. They made themselves even later by stopping to argue.

'It went fastest with me on it,' boasted Barry.

'What do you mean by fastest?' asked Chung.

'It swung from one side to the other more often,' he replied impatiently.

'It's only because you're heavier,' said Josette. 'Anything swings faster with a heavier lump on.'

'It's because Chung pulled you further over,' said Shona. 'It swings faster when each swing from side to side goes through a bigger angle.'

'I reckon it's because I stayed on longer – it gets faster the more swings you have,' said Barry.

Barry's talking nonsense,' said Chung. 'I'm sure we all swung at the same speed. But that swing is a really good one – it's got the longest rope of any swing round here. I bet that's what makes it so fast.'

Discuss

In the passage there are four ideas about swinging.
▶ Find each person's **hypothesis**.
▶ Discuss the hypotheses with your group. Decide whether each hypothesis is likely to be right, or if you are not sure.
▶ Before you do any practical work, write down the hypothesis which seems most likely to be correct. If you think they are all wrong, write down your *own* hypothesis.

Plan

Test each hypothesis in turn. You will be **experimenting**. Write down each hypothesis before you test it, and write down the results before you go on to the next one. To test each hypothesis you will need to change the pendulum in *one* way.

Set up the pendulum.

Start by changing the angle of swing. Use a protractor to measure the different angles.

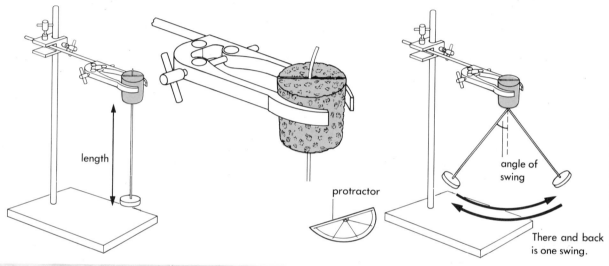

length

protractor

angle of swing

There and back is one swing.

◆ Is it more accurate to time ten swings rather than one?

Now test the other three hypotheses. Remember to change only one variable at a time.

▶ Test any other variables which might affect the rate of swing.

Record

▶ Make tables or graphs to show the results of your experiments.
▶ Write down each hypothesis and decide whether or not your results support each one. You will need to **interpret** your results carefully.

Discuss

▶ How do you think knowledge of pendulums is **applied** in the design of pendulum clocks?

Timers

Discuss

▶ How accurately can you guess one minute? Think of ways to test this.
▶ Make a list of five things which need to be timed accurately.
▶ What devices might you use to time each one?
▶ How do you think the clock below works? You are **interpreting** the photograph.

Water clocks

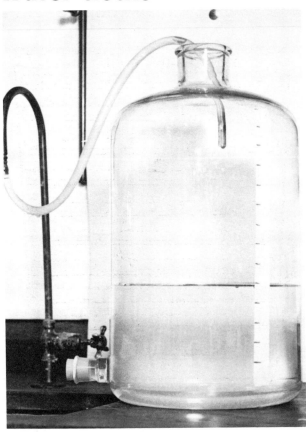

Plan

Make a water clock that will measure 30 minutes.
Decide how to record the height of water each minute.

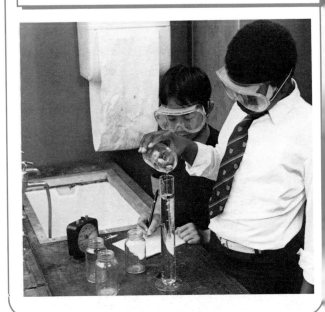

Record

▶ Draw a large labelled diagram to show how you made your clock.

Record

▸ Find out about the 'clepsydra' by doing Cut Out TM8.

Plan

Design your own clepsydra which measures 30 minutes. You will be **applying** the information you have already gathered. Check your design with your teacher before you start.

Other timers

People have made many different types of timers and clocks. The Chinese and the Romans had water clocks over two thousand years ago. There are also clocks which use other flowing materials to measure time. Sand is one of these materials. It is cheap and flows easily when it is dry. Many different civilizations have used sand-timers and sand-glasses.

Discuss

▶ Where have you seen sand-timers used?
▶ What other timing devices have you seen that depend on the flow or movement of material?
▶ How do the timers below work?

Plan

Design a hand-made clock which measures one minute. You will be **applying** what you know.
Here are some examples of things you could use: sand, flour, marbles, rice, couscous, ball-bearings.

Record

▶ Write down your results so that another group could follow what you have done.

Timing chemical reactions

Some chemicals react with each other and change colour. The colour change takes a different time depending which chemicals you use.

Plan

⚠️In this activity you are going to time a chemical reaction.

Put into a flask: 50 cm³ of liquid A, 50 cm³ of liquid B, and enough water to half fill the flask.
Add five drops of liquid C.

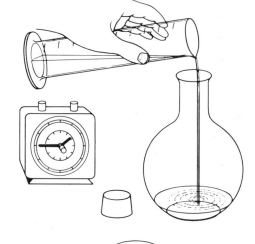

- ◆ What happens to the colour when you shake the flask?
- ◆ What happens when you leave the mixture to stand?
- ◆ Does the number of shakes make a difference to the time taken for the colour to go?

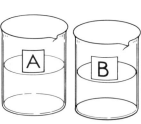

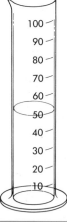

- ◆ Does anything else make a difference to the time the colour takes to go?

Test other variables which might affect how quickly the colour goes.

Discuss

▶ Discuss your **observations**.
▶ What ideas do you have to explain what you have seen?
   These ideas are your **inferences**.

Plan

Test some of your group's inferences.
You will be **experimenting**.

Record

▶ Record what you did.
▶ Record what you found out. You might like to make a table of your results.

Designing a chemical clock

Follow the plan

This reaction gives the opposite result to the first one! After the test tube has been left for a time, a blue colour should appear.

You will need lots of clean test tubes and a rack to fit them in. You also need solutions D, E, F, and G, and dropping-pipettes for each. Do not mix up the dropping-pipettes during your **investigation**.

Add two pipettes-full of D.
Add four drops of E.
Add one pipette-full of F.
Add one pipette-full of G and shake the mixture. Start timing straight away.

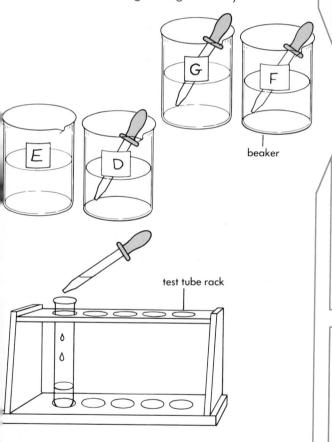

beaker

test tube rack

Time how long it takes for the blue colour to appear.

Try the reaction with different amounts of E (try one pipette-full, half a pipette-full, or four pipettes-full). Use a clean test tube each time.

Try altering the amount of F or G (try half a pipette-full, two pipettes-full, or four pipettes-full). Use a clean test tube each time.

▶ Design a chemical clock to time two minutes. You are **applying** what you have found out.

Record

▶ Describe how you made your chemical clock.
▶ Describe how accurate it was.

Time—some useful words

acceleration

afternoon

allegro

analogue

annual

antediluvian

antique

beat

birth

biennial

birthday

break

British Summer Time

bronze age

calendar

chronology

chronometer

clock

day

death

decade

dial

digital

diurnal

eon

eternity

evening

future

generation

Greenwich Mean Time

Hertz

historical

horology

hour

interval

jubilee

kilometres per hour

knot

life sentence

lifetime

lunchtime

Mach number

medieval

menstrual

miles per hour

millennium

minute

month

morning

new

night

old

paleontologist

past

pause

pendulum

perennial

period

pulse

prehistoric

present

pro tempore

rate

rhythm

season

second

shift

speed

stone age

sundial

tempo

tempus fugit

term

time fuse

timekeeper

time limit

timer

time-scale

time-switch

timetable

time zone

velocity

veteran

watch

year

young

zero hour